Tell us a story

Tell us a story

L. G. Alexander

Longman

Longman Group Limited
London

Associated companies, branches and represen-
tatives throughout the world.

First published 1972
New impression 1974
ISBN 0 582 55225 7

Printed in Hong Kong by
Wing Tai Cheung Printing Co. Ltd.

Contents

To the Teacher

This collection of stories has been reprinted from the Teacher's Books 1-4 that accompany the course *Look, Listen and Learn!* This course is intended for children aged 8/10 – 12/14 who are learning English as a foreign language. The stories follow the same structural grading scheme of *Look, Listen and Learn!* and are intended for aural comprehension. The characters referred to (Sandy, Sue, Billy, etc.) appear in the main course.

'Tell us a story!' is one of the most frequent demands made by young children (and not only young children!) but few teachers have the skill to meet this demand if they know they must tell a story within a strictly defined structural and lexical framework. It was this consideration that led to the decision to issue these stories as a separate publication because there is such an extreme shortage of suitable structurally graded material generally available. Some of the stories are also available on tape, and these are indicated in the contents list by asterisks. It goes without saying that children can only be expected to understand and enjoy stories that are read to them if they are familiar with the structural and lexical content. They are often deprived of this pleasure because stories of this kind are so hard to come by. Though these stories closely follow the grading system of a particular course, they may be used in conjunction with any other published course where there is an obvious need for material of this kind simply because most beginners courses tend to cover much the same ground.

How to use this book

The original intention was that the teacher should read stories to their classes at regular intervals during the final 5-10 minutes of an ordinary lesson. The stories were intended for pure enjoyment and no language exercises were attached to them. This continues to be the prime purpose of these stories. Words or structures known to be outside the pupils' range should be explained (and perhaps written on the blackboard) before a story is actually read. Words appearing in italics in the stories are likely to be unfamiliar to the learner and can be picked out rapidly by the teacher.

These stories can be put to a variety of obvious uses. For instance, teachers may ask comprehension questions after reading a story or they may devise simple listening comprehension tests. Alternatively, the book may be used as a reader. Whatever use is made of the material it is important not to lose sight of its basic purpose to give pleasure and enjoyment and to provide a relief from more intensive language practice.

Where's Billy?

Billy is having a birthday party, and the children there are enjoying themselves.

They are playing games.

'Let's play hide-and-seek now,' Sue says.

'All right, Sue,' the children answer.

'Count up to ten,' Billy says,

'and we can hide.'

Now Sue is counting up to ten.

'One, two, three, four . . .'

The children are running into all the *rooms*.

Some children are *hiding* in Billy's room.

They are hiding under Billy's *bed*.

Some children are hiding in the *kitchen*.

They are hiding behind the refrigerator.

Some children are hiding in the *living-room*.

They are hiding behind the door.

Sue is still counting.

'. . . five, six, seven, eight, nine, ten!' she says.

'I'm ready,' she shouts.

'I'm coming!'

The children are very quiet.

'Where are they?' Sue asks.

Now she is *looking for* them.

She is looking in Billy's *bedroom*.

She is looking under the bed.

'I can see you Sandy,' she says.

'I can see you Tom.

You're under Billy's bed.'

Now she is looking in the kitchen.

She is looking behind the refrigerator.

'I can see you Liz,' Sue says.

'I can see you Lillie.

You're behind the refrigerator.'

Now she is looking in the living-room.

She is looking behind the door.

'I can see you Tony,' Sue says.

'I can see you Sally.

You're behind the door.'

Now the children are all together.

'Where's Billy?' they ask.

'He isn't in his room,' Sue says.
'And he isn't in the kitchen,
and he isn't in the living-room.'
'Let's *find* him,' Sandy says.
The children are looking for him,
but they can't find him.
'That's funny,' Tom says.
'Let's go into the *dining-room*.'
Now Billy's mother is coming into the dining-room.
Her name is Mrs Briggs.
'What's the matter, children?' Mrs Briggs asks.
'We can't find Billy,' Sue says.
Now Sandy is looking at the table in the dining-room.
He can see a plate and some lemonade.
'Whose is this cake and this lemonade?' he asks.
'They're Billy's,' Mrs Briggs says.
'I can find Billy now,' Sandy says.
'How?' Sue asks.
'Watch me.'
Now Sandy shouts:
'I can eat Billy's cake
and drink his lemonade!'
Billy can *hear* Sandy.
'Don't eat my cake
and don't drink my lemonade,' Billy shouts.
'Don't touch them!'
'He's over there,' Sue shouts.
'He's hiding under the table!'
'That's a clever *trick*, Sandy,' Mrs Briggs says.

Tea-time

It's three o'clock.
Sue is in the kitchen.
She is helping mother.
Mother is making cakes.
'Give me some milk please, Sue,' mother says.
'There's some in that bottle.
And give me some sugar please.

There's some in that bowl.
And bring me two eggs please.
There are some in the refrigerator.'
'Yes, Mum,' Sue says. 'Here you are.'
'Thank you, Sue,' mother says.
'Now we can make some cakes.'
Mother and Sue are very busy.
They are making cakes.
Now it is nearly four o'clock.
The cakes are ready.
Sandy, Sue's brother, is coming into the kitchen.
'Mm!' he says. 'They're nice cakes.'
'Don't touch them, Sandy,' mother says.
'You can eat some cakes with your tea,
but you can't eat any now.
They're still hot.'
But Sandy isn't paying attention to mother.
He is taking a cake.
He is putting it all into his mouth.
'Oh!' he shouts.
'What's the matter?' mother asks.
'It's very hot,' Sandy says.
'Don't touch those cakes, Sandy,' mother says.
'Go out of the kitchen at once.'
'Oh, all right,' Sandy says.
'Now Sue,' mother says, 'we can make the tea.'
Mother and Sue are making the tea.
Sue is putting some hot water in the tea-pot.
Now she is taking the tea-pot and the tea-cups
into the dining-room.
'Where's father?' mother asks.
'He's upstairs,' Sue says.
'Jim!' mother shouts.
'Tea's ready!'
'I'm coming,' father answers.
Father's coming *downstairs*.
Now he's in the dining-room.
Mother, Sandy and Sue are in the dining-room,
    too.
'Mm,' father says. 'Those cakes are nice.

You're a clever girl, Sue.'

'Sue can't make cakes,' Sandy says.

'Yes, I can,' Sue says.

'No, you can't,' Sandy says.

'You can only eat them,' Sue says.

'Be quiet, children,' mother says.

Now father's looking at the table.

'I can't see any sugar,' he says.

'Bring some sugar for your father, Sandy,' mother says.

'There's some in the kitchen.'

'All right,' Sandy says.

Now Sandy's in the kitchen.

'I can't find any sugar,' he shouts.

'It's on the table,' mother says.

'I can't see it,' Sandy shouts.

'It's on the table.

It's in front of you,' mother says.

Now Sandy is coming back to the dining-room.

'Here you are dad,' he says.

'Here's the sugar.'

'Thank you, Sandy,' father says.

Now father's putting some sugar into his tea.

Now he's tasting his tea.

'Ugh!' he says. 'This tea's not very nice.'

'What's the matter with it?' mother asks.

'Taste it,' father says.

'Oh, it's nasty,' mother says.

'My tea's funny, too,' Sue says.

'I can't drink it.'

Now mother's tasting her tea.

'My tea's funny, too,' she says.

Father is looking at Sandy
and he's laughing.

'Sandy,' father says, 'taste this sugar please.'

Father is giving Sandy the bowl of sugar.

Now Sandy is tasting it.

'Ugh!' he says.

'This isn't sugar. It's *salt*.'

The Postman and the Dog

Sandy and Sue are going to school.
They are *walking* along the street.
'Look!' Sandy says.
'There's a man standing near that gate.
Who is it?'
'It's Mr Jones, the postman,' Sue says.
'He's standing in front of Mrs Mopp's house.'
'Mrs Mopp's house!' Sandy says. 'Oh dear!'
Mrs Mopp is not a nice lady.
She is very tall and very ugly.
And her house is not a nice house.
It is very big and very *dark*.
Her gate is shut
and Mr Jones can't open it.
'Listen!' Sandy says.
'Can you hear Mrs Mopp's dog?'
'Yes,' Sue answers. 'He's *barking*.'
Mrs Mopp's dog is very big.
His name is Boxer.
His face is ugly
and his teeth are long and *sharp*.
He is a nice dog,
but he *doesn't like* Mr Jones, the postman.
Now Sandy and Sue are near Mrs Mopp's house.
'Good morning, Mr Jones,' the children say.
'Good morning, Sandy.
Good morning, Sue,' Mr Jones says.
Mr Jones is standing near the gate.
He is holding a letter,
but he can't open the gate.
Boxer is standing near the gate, too,
and he's still barking.
Mr Jones's face is red.
His bag is full of letters and it is heavy.
Mr Jones is tired.
He is looking at Boxer,
and Boxer is looking at him.
Boxer's mouth is open
and Mr Jones is looking at Boxer's sharp teeth.
'What's the matter, Mr Jones?' Sandy asks.

5

'Look at that silly dog,' Mr Jones says.
'This letter is for Mrs Mopp,
but I can't give it to her.
I can't open this gate.
I can't go to Mrs Mopp's house.
I can't put this letter in her letter-box.
Be quiet!' he shouts,
but Boxer is still barking.
'Boxer's a good dog
and he's clever, too,' Sandy says.
'A good dog!' Mr Jones says.
'Look at him.
He's not a good dog.
He's a big ugly dog.
And he's nasty, too.'
'Quiet, Boxer!' Sandy says.
Now Boxer is looking at Sandy.
He isn't barking now.
'Good boy, good boy,' Sandy says.
'Give Mrs Mopp's letter to me,' Sandy says.
'All right, Sandy,' Mr Jones says.
Now Sandy is giving the letter to Boxer.
'Take this letter to Mrs Mopp, Boxer,' Sandy
    says.
Boxer is holding the letter between his teeth
and he's taking it to the house.
'Look at him, Mr Jones,' Sandy says.
'He's a good dog.'
'You're right, Sandy,' Mr Jones says.
'He's a good postman, too.
Thank you very much.'
'It's all right, Mr Jones,' Sandy says.
'Goodbye.'
'Goodbye, children,' Mr Jones answers.

At the Butcher's

'What are you doing, mum?' Sue asks.
'I'm making my shopping-list,' mother says.
'We want some beans, some potatoes,
some tomatoes, some carrots and some fruit.'

'Don't forget some bananas, mum,' Sue says.

'All right,' mother says.

'I can buy some bananas for you and Sandy.'

'Thanks, mum,' Sue says.

'Now look in the refrigerator please,' mother says.

'Is there any meat in the refrigerator?'

'No, there isn't,' Sue says.

'The refrigerator is empty.'

'Let's go to the *butcher's* shop,' mother says.

'We can buy some meat.'

Now mother and Sue are going to the butcher's
   shop.

Mrs Mopp is in the butcher's shop.

Her big dog, Boxer, is with her, too.

Mrs Mopp is buying some meat.

'I want a nice piece of meat for my *dinner*,' Mrs
   Mopp says,

'and I want some bones for my dog, Boxer.

Boxer likes bones.'

'Yes, Mrs Mopp,' the butcher says,

'a nice piece of meat and some bones for Boxer.'

Now mother and Sue are going into the butcher's
   shop.

'There's Mrs Mopp,' Sue says.

'Good morning, Mrs Mopp,' mother says.

'How are you this morning?'

'I'm not very well,' Mrs Mopp says.

'Give me some meat quickly,' Mrs Mopp says to
   the butcher.

'You're very slow this morning.'

'Yes, Mrs Mopp,' the butcher says.

The butcher is cutting a piece of meat

and he is showing it to Mrs Mopp.

'This is a nice piece of meat,' he says.

'I want that piece for my dinner,' Mrs Mopp says.

Now the butcher is putting the meat

in a piece of paper.

Now he is giving the meat to Mrs Mopp.

Mrs Mopp is putting the meat in her basket.

She is holding her basket in her right hand.

Now Boxer is looking at the basket.
Now he is putting his nose in the basket.
Mrs Mopp can't see him.
Now Boxer is going out of the shop
and he is taking the meat with him.
Now he is eating the meat.
Mrs Mopp is *paying* her bill
and she can't see Boxer.
But now she is looking in her basket.
'Where's my meat?' she asks.
'My basket's empty.'
Now Mrs Mopp is looking at the butcher.
'Give me my meat,' she says.
'It's in your basket, Mrs Mopp,' the butcher says.
'No, it's not!' Mrs Mopp shouts.
'Look!'
'That's funny,' the butcher says.
Sue is laughing.
'Look, Mrs Mopp!' Sue shouts.
'Your dog is eating the meat.'
'Oh!' Mrs Mopp shouts.
'Boxer! Bring the meat here!'
But Boxer isn't listening to her.
He's still eating.
'You can't eat that piece of meat now,' mother
    says.
'Boxer is eating it.'
'He's eating my dinner,' Mrs Mopp says.
'Never mind, Mrs Mopp,' the butcher says.
'You can eat Boxer's dinner.
You can make some nice soup with the bones!'

Chalky   It is early.
Billy and Sandy are going to school.
Billy is opening his schoolbag.
'Look, Sandy,' Billy says.
'What is it, Billy?' Sandy asks.
'It's a box,' Billy answers.
'I can see that, silly,' Sandy says.

'What's in it?'

Billy is opening the box.

'Look,' he says.

'It's a little white *mouse*.'

'It's very pretty,' Sandy says.

'What's its name?'

'Chalky,' Billy says.

'Chalky the white mouse.'

'Give me the mouse, Billy,' Sandy says.

'I want to hold it.'

'Hullo, Chalky,' Sandy says.

'Put him in the box now please, Sandy,' Billy says.

'And please be careful.'

Now Billy and Sandy are near their school.

'Listen,' Sandy says.

'That's the school bell.

Let's hurry, Billy.

We're always late."

'Look! There's Simon,' Billy says.

'He's never late.'

Sandy and Billy are running to school.

Now they are in the playground.

Now they are getting into line.

Now they are going into the classroom.

Now they are in the classroom.

Now they are standing beside their desks.

'Good morning, children,' says Miss Williams,
their teacher.

'Good morning, Miss Williams,' the children
answer.

'Sit down, children,' Miss Williams says.

'Now look at the blackboard.

This is a map of the world.

This country is France.

The capital city of France is Paris . . .'

Simon is listening to Miss Williams.

He's always well behaved.

He's never naughty.

But Sandy and Billy aren't paying attention to
Miss Williams.

They're playing with Chalky.
Billy is holding the box under the desk
and Sandy is looking at it.
Now Sandy is opening his schoolbag.
He's taking out a sandwich.
'What's that?' Billy *whispers*.
'It's a cheese sandwich,' Sandy whispers.
'Does Chalky like cheese?'
'Oh yes,' Billy answers, 'he likes cheese.'
'Here! Give him a piece,' Sandy says.
'Oh! Be careful, Sandy,' Billy says.
'Oh dear!' Sandy says.
Chalky is jumping out of the box
and is running across the classroom.
'Sandy! Billy!' Miss Williams shouts.
'What's happening?
What are you doing?'
But now she can see Chalky.
Chalky is running to her.
'Oh!' she shouts and she jumps on to a chair.
'Pick up that mouse quickly, Billy,' she says.
'I don't like *mice*.'
'I'm sorry, Miss Williams,' Billy says.
Miss Williams is *cross* with Sandy and Billy.
'Don't bring that mouse to school *again*,' she says.
'Now sit quietly and pay attention.'
Sandy and Billy are not whispering now.
They are paying attention to Miss Williams.
They are looking at the map of France.
But what's Chalky doing?
He's in his box,
and he's eating Sandy's nice cheese sandwich.

Billy's Cap   'Listen! That's the school bell,' Billy says.
'Put your books in your bags,' Miss Williams says.
'Now get into line please.
You can all go home now.'
The children are going out of the classroom.
Now they are in the playground.

'I don't want to go home now,' Billy says.
'Let's go to the lake.
Do you want to come, Sandy?'
'Yes,' Sandy says, 'I want to come.'
'I want to come, too,' Tom says.
The lake is near the school
and the boys are going there quickly.
Now they are near the lake.
'We can play football,' Billy says.
'Where's your football, Sandy?'
'It's at school,' Sandy says.
'Never mind,' Billy says.
'We can play with my cap.'
Now the boys are playing beside the lake.
Billy is throwing his cap to Tom.
'*Catch* it, Tom,' he shouts.
Tom is catching it.
Now Tom is throwing it to Sandy.
'Catch it, Sandy,' he shouts.
Sandy is catching it.
Now Sandy is throwing it to Billy.
'Catch it, Billy,' he shouts.
Billy is jumping, but he can't catch it.
'Look out, Billy!' Tom shouts.
'Your cap's *falling* into the lake!'
'Oh dear,' Billy says.
'What can I do now?'
Billy is trying to *get* his cap.
He is putting his hand into the water.
'Be careful, Billy,' Sandy says.
'Don't fall into the lake!'
'I can't get it,' Billy says.
'Here's a big stick,' Tom says.
The boys are trying to get the cap,
but they can't.
'What can we do?' Billy asks.
The boys can see a man and a dog.
The man is standing near the lake
and he is watching the boys.
'What's the matter, boys?' the man asks.

11

'My cap's in the water,' Billy says,
'and I can't get it.'
'Let me try,' the man says.
'Give me that stick.'
The man is trying, but he can't get the cap.
'Just a minute,' the man says.
'My dog, Rex, can get it for you.
Jump in, Rex,' the man says.
'Get that cap.'
Rex is jumping into the water.
Now Rex is swimming to the cap.
Now Rex is holding the cap between his teeth.
Now he is swimming back.
He is bringing Billy's cap.
'Thank you very much,' Billy says.
'It's all right,' the man answers.
Billy is looking at his cap.
'I can't put my cap on now,' Billy says.
'It's very wet.'
Billy is putting the cap in his schoolbag.
Now the boys are going home.
Now Billy is at home.
'Hullo, mum,' he says.
'Hullo, Billy,' his mother answers.
'Where's your cap?' she asks.
'It's in my bag,' Billy says.
Mother is opening Billy's bag.
'Billy!' she says.
'Look at your cap! It's wet!
And all your books are wet, too!
You are a silly boy sometimes!'

**A Quiet
Week-end**

'There's a man at the door,' Sue says.
'Who is it, Sue?' mother says.
'Open the door.'
Sue opens the door.
'It's the postman,' Sue says.
'Good morning, Sue,' the postman says.
'Here's a letter for your mother.'

'Thank you, postman,' Sue says.

Sue shuts the front door.

'Here's a letter for you, mum,' she says.

Mother takes the letter and opens it.

'It's from *Aunt* Sophie,' mother says.

'Listen! Aunt Sophie writes:

"I can come to your house for the *week-end*.

I can spend a nice quiet week-end with you.

Please meet me at the *station*.

My train arrives at twenty past four." '

'Oh, good!' Sandy says.

'Aunt Sophie is coming.

I like Aunt Sophie.'

'I like Aunt Sophie, too,' Sue says.

On Saturday, father, mother and the children

go to the station.

The train arrives at twenty past four.

'Look!' Sandy shouts.

'There's Aunt Sophie!'

'I can't see her,' Sue says.

'There she is,' Sandy says.

'She's holding two *parcels*.'

'Hullo, Aunt Sophie,' the children shout,

and they *wave* to her.

Aunt Sophie sees them and waves to them.

Then Aunt Sophie comes to them.

'Hullo, Betty,' she says to mother.

'Hullo, Jim,' she says to father.

'Hullo, children,' she says

and she *kisses* them.

'These presents are for you.

The big parcel is for Sandy

and the small parcel is for Sue.

'Oh, thank you, Aunt Sophie,' the children say.

'Can we open them now?'

'No,' father says, 'you can open them at home.'

'Come on, Sophie,'

They all go to father's car.

Father drives them all home.

'I want a nice, quiet week-end!' Aunt Sophie says.

'What's in your parcel, Sue?
Can you *guess*?' Sandy asks.
'No, can you?' Sue asks.
'No,' Sandy says, 'but it's very big.'
Now father stops the car and they all get out.
They all go into the house.
'You can open your parcels now,' father says.
Sandy opens his parcel quickly.
'Look! Look!' he says.
'What is it?' Sue asks.
'It's a *tin drum*.
What's in your parcel, Sue?'
Sue opens her parcel.
'It's a *tin whistle*.'
'They're very nice presents,' the children say,
'thank you, Aunt Sophie.'
Sandy *bangs* his tin drum
and Sue blows her tin whistle.
'Quiet!' father shouts.
'Go into the garden.'
Father puts his hands over his ears,
and the children go into the garden.
Sandy bangs his tin drum
and Sue blows her tin whistle.
'Quiet!' the *neighbours* shout.
'Go into your house!'
The neighbours put their hands over their ears
and the children go into the house.
Sandy bangs his tin drum
and Sue blows her tin whistle.
'Quiet, please, children!' Aunt Sophie says.
'I want a quiet week-end!'
Father laughs.
'You can't give Sandy a tin drum
and Sue a tin whistle
and want a quiet week-end, too!' he says.
Mother, father and Aunt Sophie
put their hands over their ears
and Sandy bangs his tin drum
and Sue blows her tin whistle!

A Thousand Pieces

Father can't fix the clock.
All the pieces are on the kitchen table
and father can't put them together.
Mother is cross with father.
She takes all the pieces
and puts them in a paper bag.
She goes to the watchmaker's.
The watchmaker's name is Mr Spink.
'Good morning, Mr Spink,' mother says.
'Good morning, Mrs Clark,' Mr Spink says.
'My clock doesn't work,' mother says.
'Can you fix it please?'
'Where is the clock?' Mr Spink asks.
'It's here,' mother says, 'in this bag.'
She gives the bag to Mr Spink.
Mr Spink opens the bag.
He sees all the pieces and laughs.
'This isn't a clock!' he says.
'I can see a thousand pieces!'
'Can you put them all together please?'
mother asks.
'I can try,' Mr Spink says.
'Come again next Tuesday.'
'Thank you, Mr Spink,' mother says
and she goes home.
Father is at home.
'Can the watchmaker fix the clock?' he asks.
'Yes,' mother says.
'I'm going to go to the watchmaker's again
on Tuesday.'
On Tuesday afternoon
mother goes to Mr Spink's shop.
'Is my clock ready?' mother asks.
'Your clock?' Mr Spink says. 'Oh, yes!'
'I can't put the pieces together.
All the pieces aren't here.'
'Oh dear,' mother says.
'Ask Mr Clark,' the watchmaker says.
'Perhaps he can give you some pieces.'
Mother goes home.

In the evening,
father comes home from work.
'Is the clock ready?' he asks.
'No,' mother says.
'Where are all the pieces?'
They look on the floor, but they can't find them.
They look in the kitchen
and in the dining-room, but they can't find them.
'That's funny,' father says.
'Perhaps they're in your pocket,' mother says.
Father looks in his pocket.
'Oh dear,' he says, 'there are three pieces here!'
'Give them to me,' mother says,
'I'm going to take them to Mr Spink.'
Mother goes to the watchmaker's the next day.
'Here you are, Mr Spink,' she says.
'Here are three pieces.'
'Thank you Mrs Clark,' Mr Spink says.
'I can fix your clock now.'
Mother *waits* and Mr Spink fixes the clock.
'It's ready now,' Mr Spink says.
'Thank you very much,' mother says,
and she pays the bill.
Mother goes home
and shows the clock to father.
'That's nice,' father says.
'The clock works now.'
Then mother and father go into the kitchen.
Mother opens the refrigerator.
'Oh dear!' she says.
'What's the matter?' father asks.
'Look at the refrigerator!' mother says.
'It doesn't work!'
'Let me fix it,' father says.
'I can fix it.'
'No, you can't,' mother says.
'You can't fix a clock
and you can't fix a refrigerator!
I don't want a thousand pieces on the floor!
Who's going to put the pieces together?'

'What are you going to do?' father asks.
'I'm going to *call an electrician!*' mother says.

On the Way to School

It is Monday morning.
Sandy and Sue are going to school.
They are walking quickly.
The holidays are over.
It's the first day of school today.
They don't want to be late.
'Oh!' Sue *cries*, 'What a rush!'
On the way to school, they meet Billy and Tom.
'Hullo, Billy! Hullo, Tom!' Sandy and Sue say.
'Hullo, Sandy! Hullo, Sue!' Billy and Tom say.
They all walk together.
There are some photographs in Sandy's schoolbag.
They are photographs of Sandy and Sue.
They are photographs of their holiday at the seaside.
Sandy wants to show the photographs to Billy and Tom.
He takes them out of his schoolbag.
'Look at these photographs of our holiday, Billy,' he says.
'Show them to me!' Billy says.
'Pass them to Billy, Sue,' Sandy says.
Sue passes Billy the photographs.
Billy looks at them and laughs.
'They're funny photographs,' he says.
'Look at this one! Look at Sandy!
You can see his head, but you can't see his *body*.
He's sitting in a big *hole* in the *sand*.
I like this photograph,' Billy says.
'Let me see it please, Billy,' Tom says.
'No,' Billy cries.
'Please let me see it, Billy.'
'No,' Billy cries.
Just then, they pass a letter-box.
'I'm not going to let you see it,' Billy says.
'I'm going to put it in this letter-box.'

'Don't do that, Billy,' Tom says.
'That's Sandy's photograph.
It isn't your photograph.'
But Billy doesn't listen to Tom.
He puts his hand in the letter-box.
Then he takes his hand out of the letter-box.
The photograph isn't in his hand.
'Where's my photograph, Billy?' Sandy shouts.
Sandy is very *cross*.
Billy laughs. 'It's in the letter-box,' he says.
Sue is cross, too.
'That's a silly *trick*,' she says.
'Give Sandy his photograph, Billy,' Sue cries.
'I can't,' Billy answers. 'It's in the letter-box.'
'Billy,' Sue says, 'you always do silly *things*.'
'What can we do now?' Tom asks.
'We can't open the letter-box,' Sandy says.
'We can't *wait* here,' Sue says.
'It's late. It's nearly time for school.'
'Oh, Billy!' Sandy cries. 'I don't like you.'
Sandy is very cross and he *pushes* Billy.
Billy pushes Sandy.
'Now don't fight!' Sue cries.
'Look! I can see a postman.
He's coming here.
Perhaps he's going to open the letter-box.'
The postman arrives at the letter-box.
'What's the matter, children?' he asks.
'My photograph is in there,' Sandy says.
'I can get it for you,' the postman says.
'I'm going to open the letter-box now.
I'm going to take out all the letters.'
The postman opens the letter-box and sees the
    photograph.
'Here you are, young man!' he says.
'Thank you very much,' Sandy answers.
The children go to school quickly. It's late.
'I'm sorry, Sandy,' Billy says.
'It's all right, Billy,' Sandy says,
'but please don't do that *again!*'

Professor Boffin Comes Home Late

It is eleven o'clock at night.

It is very late.

Professor Boffin is coming home from work.

Professor Boffin is a very clever scientist, but he often forgets things.

He often forgets the time.

He often comes home late.

The professor is walking down the street.

He is holding his umbrella and his bag.

There are very few *people* in the street.

Professor Boffin arrives home at half past eleven.

The street is very quiet.

The house is dark.

Mrs Boffin is fast asleep.

Professor Boffin opens the gate and walks to the front door.

He puts his hand in his right pocket.

Then he puts his hand in his left pocket.

Then he opens his bag and looks in it.

'That's funny!' he says. 'I can't *find* my *keys*.'

Professor Boffin usually puts his keys in his pocket, but they aren't there now!

'Oh dear!' he says.

'What am I going to do?

I don't want to *ring the bell*.

I don't want to wake up my wife.'

The professor looks up at the windows.

His bedroom window is open.

'Good!' he cries.

'The bedroom window is open.

I can get a ladder and I can *climb* through the window.

There's a ladder in the *garden* behind the house.'

Professor Boffin goes into the garden behind his house

and *fetches* a ladder.

He brings it to the front of the house

and puts it under the window.

'Now,' the professor says.

'I can climb up the ladder and climb through the

window.'

Professor Boffin climbs up the ladder.

There's a policeman opposite Professor Boffin's house.

He doesn't know Professor Boffin and he is watching him.

The policeman walks across the street.

'Hey! What are you doing?' he calls.

Professor Boffin looks down at the policeman.

'Hullo,' he says. 'I'm climbing up this ladder.'

'I can see that,' the policeman says.

'Climb down quickly

and come with me to the *police station*.'

'Oh, I'm not a *thief*,' the professor says.

'I live in this house.

I can't find my key and I'm going to climb through the window.'

'Oh no you aren't,' the policeman says.

'You're going to come with me to the police station.'

Mrs Boffin wakes up.

She can hear a *noise* and she goes to the window.

She looks out of the window.

It is very dark.

Then she sees a man on a ladder under her window!

'It's a thief!' she shouts. 'Help! Help!'

The policeman climbs up the ladder.

and pulls Professor Boffin down.

'You can't do that!' Professor Boffin shouts.

'I'm not a thief.'

Then Mrs Boffin comes downstairs and opens the front door.

'Good evening, madam,' the policeman says.

'Do you know this man?'

'Oh yes,' Mrs Boffin cries.

'It's Professor Boffin. He's my *husband*.'

'I'm very sorry, sir,' the policeman says.

'It's all right,' Professor Boffin answers. 'Good night.'

Professor Boffin goes into his house with his wife.

'What's the matter?' his wife asks.

'What's the ladder doing there under the window?'

'I can't find my keys,' the professor says.

'Look in your pockets,' Mrs Boffin says.

Professor Boffin puts his hand in his pockets *again*.

'Oh dear,' he laughs. 'The keys are in my pocket. Here they are. I'm very sorry.'

'Never mind,' Mrs Boffin says, and they both laugh.

Mrs Gasbag and the Thief

Mrs Gasbag is at home.

She is with her *friend*, Mrs Goff.

Mrs Goff often visits Mrs Gasbag.

Mrs Gasbag is a terrible gossip.

Mrs Goff is a terrible gossip, too.

Mrs Gasbag and Mrs Goff are in the *living-room*.

They are *talking* and talking and talking.

Mrs Goff is telling Mrs Gasbag a terrible story.

'There's a thief in our *neighbourhood*,' Mrs Goff says.

'He goes from house to house.

He always rides a bicycle.

He always has an empty bag in his hand.

He always stops at a house.

Then he climbs through a window.

He always fills his bag with money, then he leaves.'

'But I haven't any money,' Mrs Gasbag says.

'It doesn't matter,' Mrs Goff says.

'The thief always finds some good things in a house

and he takes them.

Be careful, Mrs Gasbag, dear. Be very careful!

He's a clever thief.'

'Oh dear,' Mrs Gasbag says.

'Don't tell me these things!'

Mrs Gasbag is very sad.

She walks across the living-room and she goes to the window.

She stops at the window and looks out.

'Mrs Goff! Mrs Goff!' she *calls*.

'Come here quickly!'

'What's the matter?' Mrs Goff asks.

'Come here quickly! Look out of the window!'
   Mrs Gasbag cries.

Mrs Goff runs to the window and looks out.

'Oh dear!' she cries. 'That's the man!'

Mrs Gasbag and Mrs Goff do not speak.

They both look out of the window.

What can they see?

They can see a man in Mrs Clark's garden.

He has a big black bag.

He is *carrying* the bag on his *shoulder*.

The bag is full and it is very heavy.

The man is leaving Mrs Clark's house.

Now he is opening the gate.

There is a bicycle near the gate.

The man is getting on his bicycle and now he is
   riding it.

Mrs Gasbag and Mrs Goff watch the man.

They are *afraid* and they don't *move*.

'What can we do?' Mrs Goff asks.

'We must call a policeman,' Mrs Gasbag cries.

'We must see Mrs Clark first,' Mrs Goff cries.

'Let's go to Mrs Clark's house at once.'

The two women go next door.

They knock at Mrs Clark's front door.

Mrs Clark opens the door.

'Hullo, Mrs Gasbag. Hullo, Mrs Goff,' she says.

'Come in. Come in.'

'We can't come in,' Mrs Gasbag says.

'We must speak to you.

There is a thief in this neighbourhood.

He always has a bag in his hand.

He has a bicycle, too.

He climbs into houses and takes money.

Then he rides away on his bicycle.'

'I don't understand,' Mrs Clark says.

Then Mrs Gasbag *tells* Mrs Clark *about* the man.

She tells her about the bag and the bicycle.
Mrs Clark listens to the story and laughs.
'That man isn't a thief,' Mrs Clark says.
'He often comes to my house.'
'But he has a big black bag,' Mrs Gasbag says.
'Of course,' Mrs Clark answers.
'His bag is full of potatoes.
He *sells* potatoes.
I always buy my potatoes from him. They're very good!'

The Dark Tunnel

It is Saturday, November 11th.
Sandy and Sue don't go to school on Saturdays.
'What can we do today, Sandy?' Sue asks.
'I don't know,' Sandy says.
Sandy goes to the window and looks out.
'What's the weather like outside?' Sue asks.
'It looks fine and dry,' Sandy says.
'Perhaps we can go for a walk,' Sue says.
'Let's ask mummy,' Sandy says.
The children go downstairs.
'Mum,' Sue says, 'we want to go for a walk.'
'It's a nice day today,' mother says,
'but it's showery weather.
Take your coats with you.'
'We don't want our coats!' Sandy says.
'All right,' mother says.
'I'm going to take my bag with me,' Sandy says.
'What's in it, Sandy?' Sue asks.
Sandy opens his bag and looks in it.
'I have lots of *useful* things in it.
I have a *pen-knife*, a torch and a map.'
'We don't need all those things!' Sue cries.
'Well, I'm going to take them with me.' Sandy answers.
'I always take my bag. It's very useful.'
'Let's go now, Sandy,' Sue says.
'We're going now, mum,' Sue calls.
'Goodbye, children,' mother says.

'Don't be late for tea.'

'No, mum,' the children say and they both leave the house.

They walk across a field.

Then they both climb a hill.

'Look down there!' Sandy says.

'Can you see those *railway-lines*?'

'Yes,' Sue answers.

'They're very old lines,' Sandy says.

'Trains don't go on them now.'

'Let's go down there,' Sue says.

Sandy and Sue run down the hill.

Suddenly Sue stops and looks up at the *sky*.

'Sandy!' she calls.

'What's the matter?' Sandy asks.

'Look at those big, black clouds!' Sue says.

'It looks showery and it feels nippy.

It's going to rain.'

'No, it isn't!' Sandy cries.

'Yes it is,' Sue says, 'and we haven't any coats.'

'Don't be silly,' Sandy says.

Just then, some big *drops* of rain *fall*.

'My goodness!' Sandy cries.

'Where can we go?' Sue asks.

'I know,' Sandy says. 'Come with me.'

Sandy runs down the hill and Sue runs after him.

'Look!' Sandy says. 'Can you see that *tunnel*?'

'Yes,' Sue answers, 'but we can't go in there.

Trains go through that tunnel.'

'They don't go through the tunnel now,' Sandy says.

'Trains don't run on these lines.'

'Then let's go in there.

It's raining very hard.' Sue says.

The children go into the tunnel.

'It's nice and dry in here,' Sandy says.

'But it's very *dark*,' Sue says. 'Turn on your torch.'

'Ha!' Sandy cries. 'Where's my useful bag?'

He opens his bag and takes out the torch.

Then he turns it on.

'Sandy!' Sue cries.

'Look! I can see two green eyes!'

'Let's go and see,' Sandy says.

'I'm not *afraid*.'

'Well, I am,' Sue says.

'Come on, Sue.'

Sue takes Sandy's hand and they go through the
tunnel.

'Look!' Sue says. 'The eyes are *moving*.'

'They're coming *towards* us. Let's run!'

'I'm not going to run!' Sandy says.

'Look!' he laughs, 'It's only a big black cat.'

The cat runs out of the tunnel

and Sandy and Sue run out of the tunnel, too.

'It's not raining now,' Sue says.

'Let's go home for tea.'

Mrs Gasbag Comes to Tea

It is four o'clock in the afternoon.

Mother is in the *kitchen*.

She is making cakes.

The children are going to come home from school
at half past four.

Suddenly, mother hears the door-bell.

'That's the children,' she says. 'They're early.'

She opens the door, but it isn't the children.

It's Mrs Gasbag.

'Good afternoon, Mrs Gasbag,' mother says.

'Good afternoon, Mrs Clark,' Mrs Gasbag says.

Mrs Gasbag often visits mother

and she stays for *hours* and hours.

'Mm,' Mrs Gasbag says. 'Those cakes smell nice.'

'Sit down, Mrs Gasbag,' mother says.

Mother brings a plate full of cakes.

'Do you want one?' she asks.

'Oh, yes please,' Mrs Gasbag says.

'Do you want a cup of tea, too?' mother asks.

'Yes, please,' Mrs Gasbag says.

Mrs Gasbag drinks tea and eats cakes

and she talks and talks and talks.

She *talks about* Professor Boffin

and she talks about Mrs Boffin

and she talks about Mrs Mopp and her ugly dog, Boxer,

and she talks about all the *neighbours*.

Now it is half past four.

Sandy and Sue come home from school.

They see Mrs Gasbag in the living-room.

'Good afternoon, Mrs Gasbag,' they say.

'Good afternoon, children,' Mrs Gasbag says.

Mother looks at Sandy.

He looks hot and tired.

'What's the matter with you, Sandy?' mother asks.

'You look hot and tired.'

'I'm all right,' Sandy says.

'Please let me eat some cakes.

They look very nice.'

'They taste very nice, too,' Sue says.

Now Mrs Gasbag talks to the children.

'What's Billy Briggs like?' she asks.

'He's funny,' Sandy says.

'What's Tom like?' Mrs Gasbag asks.

'He's clever,' Sandy says.

'What's Simon like?' Mrs Gasbag asks.

'He's well-behaved, but he's silly sometimes,' Sue says.

Mrs Gasbag talks and talks.

She asks questions about all their *friends*.

She eats lots of cakes and drinks seven cups of tea.

The time passes.

It's nearly six o'clock. Father comes home.

'Good evening, Mrs Gasbag,' he says.

'Good evening, Mr Clark,' Mrs Gasbag says.

Mrs Gasbag talks to father and the time passes.

Six o'clock, seven o'clock, eight o'clock

. . . and Mrs Gasbag is still talking!

Mother and father go into the kitchen.

'How can we *make her go?*' mother *whispers*.

'The children are very tired and Sandy isn't very well.'

'Sandy isn't very well?' father asks.

'I have an *idea*.'

Father goes into the living-room and looks at Sandy.

'You don't look very well,' he says.

'How do you feel?'

'I feel hot and tired,' Sandy says.

'He's all right,' Mrs Gasbag says.

'Open your mouth, Sandy,' father says.

'Show me your tongue.'

Then father puts his hand on Sandy's *forehead*.

'Mm,' he says, 'Sandy has a temperature.'

'Have you a headache, Sandy?' father asks.

'No,' Sandy answers, 'but I'm hot.'

'Perhaps he has measles,' father says,

'or perhaps he has mumps. He is very ill.'

Mrs Gasbag hears this.

'Measles or mumps?' she says. 'I don't want to *catch* measles and mumps. I'm going home!'

'Good night, Mrs Gasbag,' they all say.

Mrs Gasbag leaves quickly and mother and father laugh.

'What a good idea!' mother says.

'Come on children. It's time for bed. It's very late.'

What's the Matter with Billy?

Tom and Billy are going home from school.

They always pass *Farmer Gimbel's orchard* on the way home.

The orchard is full of apple trees.

And the trees are full of apples.

'Look at all those apples,' Billy says.

'I love apples. I'm going to get some.'

'You mustn't do that, Billy,' Tom says.

'Farmer Gimbel has a big dog.'

'I don't care,' Billy says and he *climbs* over the fence.

'Wait there, Tom,' he calls.

Tom waits for Billy and Billy climbs an apple tree.

'Look at all those lovely apples,' Billy says.

Billy *picks* lots and lots of apples.
He fills his pockets and he fills his schoolbag.
Farmer Gimbel doesn't see him,
and Farmer Gimbel's dog doesn't hear him.
Billy goes back to Tom.
'Look at all these apples, Tom,' Billy cries.
'Do you want any?'
'No thanks, Billy,' Tom says.
'You can't eat those apples. They're *green*.
Green apples can give you a stomach-ache.'
Billy laughs. 'I love green apples,' he says.
Billy eats eight green apples, then he goes home.
The next day, Billy doesn't go to school.
'Where's Billy today?' Miss Grant asks.
'I don't know,' Tom answers.
Of course Billy is at home.
He's in bed. He has a terrible stomach-ache.
'Billy looks very ill,' Mrs Briggs says.
'I must call the doctor.
Billy has a terrible stomach-ache.'
Mrs Briggs calls the Doctor and he comes to her
    house.
The doctor looks at Billy.
'What's the matter with him, Doctor?' Mrs
    Briggs asks.
'He has a bad stomach-ache,' the Doctor says.
'He must stay in bed.
He must drink this medicine *three times a day*.'
'Yes, Doctor,' Mrs Briggs says.

Tom and Sandy are coming home from school.
'Let's go and see Billy,' Tom says.
'Yes,' Sandy says. 'Perhaps he's ill.'
'We can take him some nice apples,' Tom says.
'Billy loves apples.'
Tom and Sandy pass Farmer Gimbel's orchard
and Tom climbs over the fence and picks some
    apples.
'You can't take those apples to Billy,' Sandy says.
'They're green.'

'It doesn't matter,' Tom says. 'Billy loves green apples.'

Tom puts eight apples in his schoolbag
and the two boys go to Billy's house.

'Good afternoon, Mrs Briggs,' Tom says.

'Where's Billy?'

'He's in bed,' Mrs Briggs says. 'He's ill.'

'Can we see him please?' Tom asks.

'Yes, come upstairs with me,' Mrs Briggs says.

Mrs Briggs and the boys go upstairs.

'Good afternoon, Billy,' Tom says.

'Ooooh!' Billy cries. 'I have a stomach-ache.'

'What's the matter?' Tom asks.

'I don't know,' Billy answers.

'I must drink this medicine. It's bitter and nasty.'

'We have a present for you,' Tom says.

He opens his schoolbag and takes out the green apples.

'Here you are, Billy, some lovely green apples.'

'Oh, I don't want any green apples,' Billy says.

Mrs Briggs sees the apples.

'Billy can't eat those apples, Tom,' she says. 'They're green.'

'But Billy always eats green apples,' Tom says.

'He eats lots and lots of green apples.'

Mrs Briggs looks at Billy. She is *cross*.

'Billy!' she cries, 'You mustn't eat green apples again.'

'I'm sorry, mum,' Billy says.

'I'm never going to eat green apples again. Ooooh!'

Father has a Bath

'Have a slice of bread and some jam, Sandy,' mother says.

'May I have some cake, please, mum?' Sue says.

'Of course, Sue,' mother says.

'May I have a cup of tea, dear?' father says.

'Of course, Jim,' mother says.

The Clarks are having their tea. It is four o'clock.

'I'm going to have a walk in the park after tea,'

29

mother says.

'Sue and I are going to come with you,' Sandy says.

'Well, I'm going to have a bath,' father says.

They all *finish* tea.

Mother and the children put on their hats and coats.

'We're going now,' mother says. 'Enjoy your bath.'

'Have a good time,' father calls. 'Goodbye.'

Mother, Sandy and Sue go to the park.

'What can we do, Sandy?' Sue asks.

'We can have a game,' Sandy shouts.

He is very happy.

A lady is sitting on a seat.

She has a baby in a pram.

'You mustn't shout like that,' the lady says to Sandy.

'My baby's having a sleep in his pram.

You mustn't wake him up.'

'I'm sorry,' Sandy says.

Sandy and Sue run across the park together.

Mother runs after them. 'Wait for me,' she calls.

Mother, Sandy and Sue are having a good time.

Father's at home.

He's having a good time, too.

He's having a bath and he's singing.

The bath is full of water.

'Ah!' father says. 'This is lovely.

Lovely hot water. Tra la-la la-la,' he sings.

Suddenly he stops and listens.

'What's that noise?' father says.

'Ting a-ling-ling, ting a-ling-ling!'

'Oh dear,' father says. 'It's the *telephone!*

What am I going to do?

I can't answer it now.'

But it *rings* and rings.

'Ting a-ling-ling, ting a-ling-ling!' It doesn't stop.

'Oh!' father cries and he gets out of the bath.

He puts a towel *round himself* and goes out of the bath-room.

He picks up the *receiver*.

'Hullo,' he says. But *no one* answers.

'That's funny!' father says.

He puts the receiver back and goes back to the bath-room.

Then he gets into the bath.

'I must have a good wash now,' father says.

He sings *again*. 'Tra la-la, la-la,' he sings.

Suddenly he stops and listens.

'Ting a-ling-ling, ting a-ling-ling!'

'Oh dear,' father says. 'It's that silly telephone again.

I can't answer it this time.

It can ring and ring.'

And of course it rings and rings and rings.

'Oh, all right!' father shouts.

He puts a towel round himself and goes out of the bath-room.

He picks up the receiver.

'Hullo! Hullo!' he says, but no one answers.

Father's very *cross*.

He puts the receiver back and goes back to the bath-room.

Then he gets into the bath again.

He sits in the water.

'This water's nearly cold,' father says. 'Never mind.

I must have a good wash now.'

Father takes some soap and sings again.

Then he stops and listens.

'Ting a-ling-ling, ting a-ling-ling.'

This time, father jumps out of the bath.

He puts a towel round himself and runs to the telephone.

He picks up the receiver.

'Hullo,' a voice says. 'Is that Mr John Shrimp?'

'Who?' father says.

'Mr John Shrimp,' the voice says.

'No!' father shouts. '*Wrong number!*'

Now he is very cross. He puts the receiver down.

Just then, mother and the children come in.

They see father with a towel round himself and
   laugh.
The mother sees all the water on the floor.
'What are you doing?' mother asks.
She is cross now. 'Look at all this water!'
'Oh dear,' father says. 'I want to have a bath.
Please let me have a bath!'

Professor Boffin Finds his Car

'Where's the key to my car, dear?' Professor
   Boffin asks.
' I can't find it.'
'You are careless!' Mrs Boffin says.
'The day before yesterday it was in this tin,
but it isn't here now.
Yesterday it was in this box, but it isn't here now.'
'And where is it today, dear?' Professor Boffin
   asks.
'Perhaps it's in your car,' Mrs Boffin says.
'I must go and see,' Professor Boffin answers.
Professor Boffin goes outside and then comes back.
He looks very sad.
'Well?' Mrs Boffin asks. 'What's the matter now?'
'Now I can't find my car!' Professor Boffin says.
'You can't find your car!' Mrs Boffin cries.
'Where were you yesterday?'
'I can't remember, dear.'
'Think! Were you at the library?'
'No, I wasn't at the library.'
'Were you at the stationer's?'
'No, I wasn't at the stationer's.'
'You weren't at the greengrocer's,
and you weren't at the grocer's, or the butcher's
   or the baker's.
Where were you?'
'I know!' Professor Boffin cries. 'I was at the
   barber's.'
'Yes, I remember,' Mrs Boffin says. 'You were at
   the barber's.
Your car is outside the barber.'s shop.

Go to the barber's and bring your car home.'

Professor Boffin goes to the barber's.

He stops outside the barber's shop and *looks for* his car,

but it isn't there.

'That's funny,' the professor says, and he goes into the barber's.

'Good morning, Professor Boffin,' the barber says.

'Do you want a haircut?'

'No, thanks,' Professor Boffin answers.

'I want my car. I can't find it.

It isn't outside your shop.'

The barber goes out of the shop with Professor Boffin.

'It isn't here,' he says. 'Where were you yesterday?'

'I was here,' Professor Boffin says.

'You were here, but your car isn't here now.'

'Oh dear,' Professor Boffin says. 'I must go home.'

He goes home *again*.

'Was your car at the barber's?' Mrs Boffin asks.

'No, it wasn't,' Professor Boffin says. 'I can't find it.'

'Well, sit down and have some tea,' Mrs Boffin says.

'Tea's ready.'

Professor Boffin sits down and has some tea.

He is very quiet.

'What's the matter?' Mrs Boffin asks.

'I'm thinking.'

'Yes,' Mrs Boffin says, 'but what's the matter?

You don't look very well.'

'I don't feel very well,' the professor says. 'I have a toothache.

This tea's very hot.'

'A toothache!' Mrs Boffin says.

'I remember now. You were

at the dentist's the day before yesterday.

Your car's outside the dentist's.'

'You're right, dear!' Professor Boffin cries and

he jumps up.

'I'm going to find it.'

Professor Boffin runs out of the house and goes to the dentist's.

He hasn't a toothache now. He's thinking of his car.

He arrives at the dentist's and sees his car.

'There's my car!' Professor Boffin cries. 'That's good!'

But there's a policeman standing beside the car.

'Is this your car, sir?' the policeman asks.

'Yes,' Professor Boffin answers.

'Well,' the policeman says. 'You must pay a lot of money.'

'Why?' Professor Boffin asks.

'Because you can't park here,' the policeman says.

'This car was here yesterday and the day before yesterday. Look,' the policeman says. 'It says "No Parking".

You can't park here, so you must pay a lot of money.'

'I never remember things,' Professor Boffin says

'A bad *memory* is very *expensive!*' the policeman answers.

The Snowman

It's a cold evening in winter.

Father comes home from work.

'My goodness!' he cries. 'It's nippy this evening! It's only five o'clock and it's dark outside.

Let's listen to the weather forecast.

It's going to snow tomorrow.

Turn on the radio, Sandy.'

Sandy turns it on.

'Here is the weather forecast for tomorrow, January 26th.

It's going to be a cold day tomorrow.

It's going to snow in the north and south.'

'Hurray!' Sue shouts. 'We're lucky!

Let's go for a walk tomorrow, dad.'

'All right, children,' father says.

Sandy and Sue get up early next morning.

'Sandy,' Sue says. 'Look out of the window.
It's beautiful!'

There was snow in the street.

There was snow in the garden and on the trees.

There was snow on the houses.

'Sue!' Sandy cries. 'We're going to have a good
time today.'

Then mother comes into the room.

'Put on very warm clothes today, children,' she
says.

'It's very cold outside.'

Father was still in bed.

'Dad! Dad!' the children shout.

'Get up now. Please get up quickly.

We want to go for a walk in the snow.'

'Brrrr! It's nippy!' father says.

He gets up and puts on warm clothes.

Then they all have breakfast and leave the house.

They all walk across the fields together.

'Your nose is red, Betty,' father laughs.

'Brrrr!' she says. 'It's freezing!

I don't like cold weather.'

Father laughs. He picks up some snow and makes
a snowball.

Then he throws it at mother.

Mother picks up some snow and throws it at
father.

Then the children make snowballs and throw
them too.

They are all enjoying the snow.

'Are you cold now?' father asks.

'No,' mother says. 'My hands were cold, but they
are warm now.'

Then Sue throws a snowball at father.

'Brrrr!' father shouts.

'What's the matter, dad?' Sue asks.

'That snowball is going under my shirt,' father
says.

'It's very cold.'

'I'm going to eat some of this snow,' Sandy says.

He picks up some snow in his hands and puts it in his mouth.

'Mm,' he cries. 'It's lovely. It's like ice-cream.'

Then Sue eats some, too.

'It is lovely,' she says, 'but it isn't like ice-cream.'

'What's it like then?' Sandy asks.

'It's like water, silly,' Sue says and laughs.

'The children are enjoying the snow,' mother says.

'We are lucky this year.

There wasn't any snow last year, but there's a lot this year.'

Then Sandy and Sue see a funny thing in the *middle* of the field.

'Look, dad,' Sandy says. 'What's that?'

'It's a snowman,' father says.

They run across the snow to the middle of the field.

'Wait for me,' mother calls. 'I can't run in this snow.'

Then they stop near the snowman.

'He's a funny snowman,' Sandy says. 'Look at his arms.'

Sandy touches the snowman and *brushes away* some snow.

'Oooh! Look!,' he cries. 'There are some clothes under this snow.'

'Oh,' mother cries. 'Perhaps it's a man!'

'A man!' father cries.

He brushes away some snow, too.

'Look! There's a hat and a coat.'

Then he laughs. 'It's not a man. It's a *scarecrow*.'

They all laugh.

'He's very cold,' father says.

'Let's make snowballs and throw them at him.'

'Ooh, let's,' the children say.

'I like winter,' Sue says.

'I like winter, too,' Sandy says.

'It's the best time of the year.'

I Can't Pay my Bill!

'Sandy,' mother said.

'Please go to the butcher's and get some meat.

Get some nice pieces of steak.

We're going to have steak for dinner tonight.'

'Don't go to the butcher's,' father said.

'Let's have a meal at a restaurant tonight.'

'May we come, too?' Sue asked.

'Of course,' father answered.

'Oh,' Sue cried, 'that's a lovely treat.'

'I'm going to have a bath,' father said, 'and then
     we can leave.'

Father had a bath.

Then he said, 'I'm ready now.'

'We're ready, too,' mother answered.

The family walked to the restaurant

because it was near their home.

It was a very big restaurant and it was very nice.

'Good evening,' the *waiter* said.

'Good evening,' they all answered.

'A table for four people, sir?' the waiter asked
     father.

'Yes please,' father said.

'Mm. I'm hungry,' Sandy said.

'What are you going to have, Betty,' father asked.

'I'm going to have some chicken,' mother said.

'And I want some potatoes and vegetables.'

'What do you want, Sue?' father asked.

'I want some chicken, too, please,' Sue said.

'What about you, Sandy?'

'I want a big steak please,' Sandy said.

'I'm going to have a steak, too,' father said.

They all enjoyed their food very much.

But the last course was the best.

Mother and father had ice-cream and coffee.

Sandy and Sue had strawberries, sugar and cream.

Sandy wanted some ice-cream, too.

'Do you like that ice-cream?' he asked his mother.

'Yes,' mother answered.

'Can I try some please?'

'All right,' mother said.

37

'I want to try some, too,' Sue said.

Sandy and Sue had a little ice-cream.

'Don't eat a lot,' mother said.

Then father looked at his watch.

'It's late,' he said. 'I must pay the bill.'

Father *waved* to the waiter.

'Do you want to have some fruit?' the waiter asked.

'No, thank you,' father said.

'I want to pay my bill.

Bring me the bill please.'

'Yes, sir,' the waiter said.

'Here you are, sir,' the waiter said.

Father looked at the bill.

'Oh, dear!' father said.

'What's the matter?' mother asked.

Father's face was very red.

'What's the matter, dad?' Sue asked.

'I can't find my *wallet*,' father said.

'You can't find your wallet!' mother cried.

'What are we going to do?

How can you pay the bill?

Look in all your pockets.'

Father looked in all his pockets again, but it wasn't
  there.

'I haven't any money with me,' mother said.

'I have my pocket-money,' Sandy said.

'Look, I have a shilling.'

Father laughed. 'That's not much,' he said.

'How can I pay the bill?' father asked the waiter.

'I can't find my wallet.

Now I must wash the plates in this restaurant
and pay my bill like that.'

The waiter looked at father, then he looked on the
  floor.

'Is this your wallet, sir?' the waiter asked.

He picked up a black wallet.

'Yes, that's it!' father cried.

'You *dropped* it a moment ago,' the waiter said.

'Thank you very much,' father said
and he paid the bill.

'Next time, be careful!' mother said.
'We all had a bad *shock!*'

Farmer Gimbel's Donkey

'Where's Sue?' mother asked.
'She was in town with grandpa,' father said,
'but she's here now.
They both arrived home a few minutes ago.'
'Mum,' Sue called. 'Mum!'
'Yes, Sue,' mother answered.
'Here we are, Betty,' grandfather said.
He smiled at mother.
'A funny thing happened on the way to town,
    mother,' Sue said.
'What happened, Sue?' mother asked.
'Well,' Sue said.
'Grandpa and I were in the street.
Then he noticed a donkey.
The donkey walked across the road.
Then it stopped in the middle of the road
and it stopped all the traffic.
It was very funny.
We laughed and laughed, but the car drivers were
    cross.'
'What happened then?' father asked.
'Then a policeman arrived,' Sue answered.
'Whose donkey was it?' mother asked.
'It was farmer Gimbel's,' grandfather answered.
'The policeman said: "You must move your
    donkey."
Then the policeman and farmer Gimbel
tried to move the donkey.
Farmer Gimbel was in front of the donkey and he
    pulled.
The policeman was behind the donkey and he
    pushed.
They worked very hard, but they didn't move the
    donkey.
The donkey didn't want to move at all!'
'That was funny,' Mother said. 'Is the donkey

still there?'

'No, mum,' Sue said.

'Grandpa said to farmer Gimbel: "Give the donkey a carrot!" '

'Did farmer Gimbel give the donkey a carrot?' father asked.

'Yes, he did,' Sue said, 'and the donkey followed him across the road.

'How did the donkey run away?' father asked.

'Well,' Sue said.

'The donkey was in a field with farmer Gimbel.

Farmer Gimbel had his cart and the donkey was going to pull it.

Farmer Gimbel opened the gate and called the donkey.

But then the donkey didn't want to pull the cart.

The donkey noticed the open gate and *went* out.

At first farmer Gimbel didn't notice.

Then he looked up, but the donkey wasn't there!

Then farmer Gimbel looked in the street
and noticed the donkey.

Farmer Gimbel called: "Come back! Come back!"

But the donkey didn't listen to him.

It went down the street.

It noticed Mrs Gasbag in the street.

Mrs Gasbag was with Mrs Boffin.

Then the donkey stopped near Mrs Gasbag and looked at her.'

'Why, Sue?' mother asked.

'Because there were some nice flowers on Mrs Gasbag's hat.

The donkey tried to eat the flowers.

It knocked Mrs Gasbag's hat on to the road.

Then it kicked Mrs Gasbag's hat.

Mrs Gasbag was very cross.

She shouted at farmer Gimbel,

and farmer Gimbel said: "I'm sorry, Mrs Gasbag."

Then the donkey walked into the middle of the road
and stopped the traffic.

There was a traffic-jam.

Mrs Gasbag went home. She was very cross.'

'*Poor* Mrs Gasbag!' mother said.

'Now she needs a new hat.'

'Farmer Gimbel must buy one for her,' Sue said.

Mrs Gasbag's Hat

Yesterday Mrs Gasbag spent the day with her friend, Mrs Goff.

Mrs Gasbag went to Mrs Goff's house early.

She knocked at the front door and Mrs Goff opened it.

'Hullo, dear,' Mrs Goff said. 'Come in and have some coffee.'

Mrs Gasbag went in. She looked very sad.

'What's the matter with you?' Mrs Goff asked.

'Where's your lovely hat?'

Mrs Gasbag *told* Mrs Goff the sad story.

'Farmer Gimbel's donkey knocked my hat on to the road.

Then he kicked it.' Mrs Gasbag said.

Now Mrs Goff was very cross.

'Farmer Gimbel must buy a new hat for you,' she said.

'Go to farmer Gimbel's and ask him for a new hat.

Take the old hat with you and show it to him.

We can go together. Let's go now.'

Mrs Gasbag and Mrs Goff first went to Mrs Gasbag's house.

Mrs Gasbag got her hat and Mrs Goff looked at it.

'My goodness!' Mrs Goff said. 'Look at it! Just look at it!'

'It's a new hat, too,' Mrs Gasbag said.

'It was a new hat,' Mrs Goff said.

'It looks old and dirty now.

The lovely red and yellow flowers are nearly black.'

'Let's go to farmer Gimbel's now,' Mrs Gasbag said.

So the two ladies went to farmer Gimbel's.

They arrived at the farm and looked over the gate.

They looked at the donkey in the field
and the donkey looked at them.

But they didn't see farmer Gimbel.

'There's the donkey!' Mrs Gasbag cried.

'Open the gate and we can go to the *farm-house*,'
Mrs Goff said.

They opened the gate and walked across the field.

The donkey noticed them and came across the
field.

Mrs Gasbag *held* her hat in her hand and the
donkey looked at it.

'Let's run,' Mrs Gasbag cried.

'That donkey wants to eat my hat again!'

The ladies *ran* across the field and the donkey ran
after them.

'Whew! I can't run *so fast*!' Mrs Goff said. 'I'm
fat!'

Then they noticed farmer Gimbel.

'*Shoo!*' farmer Gimbel shouted 'Go away you
silly donkey!'

'What?' Mrs Goff shouted. 'What did you say?'

'I'm not talking to you,' farmer Gimbel said.

'I'm talking to the donkey.'

Then Mrs Gasbag showed her hat to farmer
Gimbel.

'Look at my hat,' she said. 'It was new yesterday.'

'I'm sorry,' farmer Gimbel said. 'It was an
accident.'

'You must buy a new hat for Mrs Gasbag,' Mrs
Goff said.

'All right,' farmer Gimbel said.

'Now please go away. I'm busy.' He was very cross.

Mrs Goff and Mrs Gasbag went home.

Mrs Gasbag put her old hat into a box and *sent* it
to the farmer.

The postman took the parcel to farmer Gimbel's
house.

'What's this?' farmer Gimbel asked.

He opened the parcel.

There was a letter in it.

The letter was from Mrs Gasbag.

The letter said: 'Here is my old hat. Your donkey likes it very much, so he can have it.'

Farmer Gimbel read the letter and laughed.

Then the postman went to Mrs Gasbag's house.

He had a parcel for Mrs Gasbag.

Mrs Goff was at Mrs Gasbag's and they both opened the parcel.

'What's in it?' Mrs Goff asked.

'I don't know,' Mrs Gasbag said.

'Look! It's full of lovely flowers,' Mrs Goff said.

'These aren't flowers,' Mrs Gasbag said.

'This is a new hat.

Farmer Gimbel sent it to me.

It's just like my old one.'

'Look, there's a letter in the parcel,' Mrs Goff said.

Mrs Gasbag read the letter.

It said: 'Here is a nice new hat for you from farmer Gimbel.

Please don't go near my donkey again.

He likes hats.

He likes your hat very much and he's wearing it now.'

Mrs Gasbag and Mrs Goff laughed and laughed.

Mrs Taylor's Baby

Last week mother visited her friend, Mrs Taylor, and Sue went with her.

Sue wanted to go to Mrs Taylor's because she wanted to see Mrs Taylor's baby.

Mrs Taylor's little boy is one year old.

His name is Timmy.

He is a very pretty child.

He has soft brown hair and big blue eyes.

He always smiles and he's very happy, but sometimes he's naughty, too.

Mother and Sue arrived at Mrs Taylor's house.

Sue ran into the house. 'Where's Timmy?' she

asked.

'Sh!' Mrs Taylor said. 'Don't make a noise, Sue.
Timmy's asleep. He's not very happy today.'

'Why?' Sue asked.

'Because he has a new tooth and it hurts him a lot.'

'*Poor* Timmy!' Sue said.

Sue went into his bedroom and looked at him.

Timmy was in his *cot* and he was fast asleep.

He looked very sweet.

Then Mrs Taylor called Sue, so she went out of
Timmy's room.

'Come and have some tea, Sue,' Mrs Taylor said.

'It's nearly ready. I'm going to set the table.'

Mrs Taylor set the table and Sue and mother
helped her.

Then they all sat down and had a lovely tea.

They had sandwiches and cakes and biscuits.

Mother and Mrs Taylor drank tea, but Sue was
very lucky.

She drank some lemonade.

Then mother said, 'Let's go for a walk.'

But Mrs Taylor said, 'I can't. I don't want to take
Timmy.'

'You can both go for a walk,' Sue said.

'I can stay here and *look after* Timmy. I don't
mind.'

'Of course,' mother said. 'Sue can look after him.
Sue likes babies.'

So Mrs Taylor and mother went out for a walk.

Sue sat in the living-room and read a book.

Timmy was still asleep.

After half an hour, Timmy woke up.

Sue didn't hear him.

Timmy *climbed* out of his *cot* and *crawled* out of
his bedroom.

He went into the *dining-room*.

There were lots of things on the table.

There was a tea-pot and there were some plates
and cups.

Timmy crawled to the table and took the *table-*

cloth in his hands.

Then he pulled hard. *Crash!*

Some plates and cups *fell* on to the floor and broke.

Some cake fell on to the floor, too.

Timmy took a piece of cake and ate it.

Sue heard the noise and ran into the dining-room.

Then she saw Timmy.

'Timmy!' she called, 'you naughty boy!'

Timmy smiled at her and pulled the tablecloth
again.

'Don't!' Sue cried. 'Stop it!'

She ran to Timmy and picked him up.

Then she carried him into his bedroom.

Timmy didn't like this at all.

He *cried* and cried.

'He wants some cake,' Sue thought, 'but I can't
give him any.'

Sue gave Timmy some toys instead, but he didn't
stop.

He threw the toys on to the floor and cried.

'What can I do?' Sue said.

Then she sang to Timmy.

She sang a very nice song,

but Timmy didn't listen to it.

Then Sue saw Timmy's new tooth.

'Poor Timmy!' she said. 'It's his new tooth. It
hurts him.'

Sue put her finger into Timmy's mouth and he
bit it.

'Ouch!' Sue cried. 'You are very naughty today.'

Just then, mother and Mrs Taylor came home.

They saw the cups and plates on the floor.

Mrs Taylor hurried into Timmy's room.

'What happened?' she asked.

Sue told her about Timmy and Mrs Taylor
laughed.

'It doesn't matter, Sue,' Mrs Taylor said.

'*It wasn't your fault*. Timmy was naughty.'

'He bit my finger, too,' Sue said

and she showed Mrs Taylor her finger.

'He only has one tooth, but it's very *sharp*.'

Mother and Mrs Taylor laughed and Timmy laughed too.

Father Hangs a Picture

Father came home early the other day.

He looked very happy.

He had a big parcel under his arm.

There was some brown paper round the parcel.

Father took off the brown paper.

'Look!' he cried. 'I bought this picture today. Isn't it lovely!'

It was lovely. It was a beautiful picture.

'Oh!' mother cried. 'That's very nice.

We need a picture on the wall in the living-room.'

'Good,' father said. 'I'm going to hang it.'

Father worked very hard and the children worked hard too.

Sandy and Sue carried the ladder into the living-room.

Father *climbed* up the ladder and made a mark on the wall.

'There!' he cried. 'We can put the picture there. Is that all right?'

We looked at it.

'Yes, dad,' we said.

'Good,' father said. 'Now I haven't got a hammer and I haven't got any nails. Please bring me some.'

Sandy and Sue brought some nails and a hammer.

'Hold the ladder, Sandy,' father said.

Sandy held the ladder and father went up.

'Where's that mark?' he said. 'I can't find that mark.'

They all looked for the mark, but it wasn't there.

'That's funny,' father said. 'I must make a new mark.'

This time father made a very big mark.

'Now I can put a nail in the wall,' he said.

Father took the hammer and began to work.

Suddenly he hit his finger hard and shouted crossly.

'Ouch!' he said. 'This is a silly hammer.'

Mother laughed. 'Don't *blame* the hammer!' she said.

'You're not a very good workman.'

Father didn't answer.

His finger hurt very much.

'Do you want any sticking-plaster?' mother asked.

'Yes, please,' father said.

Sue ran and got some quickly.

Mother looked at father's finger. His *finger-nail* was black!

'My goodness!' she cried. She put some sticking-plaster round it.

'It's all right now,' father said. 'I can hang the picture now.'

Father climbed up the ladder again.

He found the mark easily this time.

The mark was very big.

Then father hit the nail with the hammer.

'That's funny,' father said.

'This nail doesn't go in easily.

Bring a big nail, Sandy.'

Sandy brought a big nail and father hit it hard.

He worked fast, but he didn't work very well.

He hit the nail for a long time and made a big hole in the wall.

Mother saw it and she was very cross.

'Look at that nice wall,' she said crossly.

'Now you must *cover* the hole with the picture.

The wall is very ugly.'

Father worked hard again.

At last he *hung* the picture on the wall.

'Do you like it?' he asked.

'It's very high now,' mother said, 'but it looks all right.

Come and have tea.'

They all went and had tea.

Then they heard a loud noise.

'What's that?' father asked.

'It's your picture, dear,' mother said.

They ran to the living-room.

'Look!' mother cried. 'The picture's on the floor! You didn't hang it very well!'

'Oh dear,' father said. 'Look at my nice new picture.

It *fell* on the floor and the glass broke and the *frame* broke.'

'We haven't got a nice new picture now,' Sue said.

'No,' mother said. 'We haven't got a nice new picture,

but we've got a nice big hole in the wall!'

The Slot Machine

'Goodness me!' Mrs Boffin said.

'I feel very hungry tonight.'

'Hungry, dear?' Professor Boffin asked.

'We've just had dinner.

You've just had some steak and potatoes and strawberries and cream!'

'I know,' Mrs Boffin said, 'but I'm still hungry.

Go and buy a bar of chocolate for me dear.'

'All right,' Professor Boffin said.

Professor Boffin put on his hat and coat and went out.

He went to Mr Hill's sweet shop, but the shop was shut.

Professor Boffin looked at his watch.

'It's late,' he said. 'The sweet shop is shut, so I can't buy any chocolate.'

Professor Boffin walked home slowly.

He stopped near the park and listened to the birds.

He stopped and looked at the *ducks*.

At last he arrived home.

'You were a long time,' Mrs Boffin said.

'Where have you been?'

'I've been to the sweet shop, dear,' Professor Boffin said.

'It's shut.'

'Go there again and knock at the door.

Mr Hill can open it for you.'

'I've already been to the sweet shop dear. Mr Hill
   isn't there.

It's late. The sweet shop is shut.'

'There's a slot machine outside Mr Hill's shop,'
   Mrs Boffin said.

'The slot machine is full of bars of chocolate.

You can buy some chocolate from the machine.'

'All right, dear, but I haven't got any change.'

'Look in my button box,' Mrs Boffin said.

'There are a few pence in there.'

Professor Boffin took some *coins* and went out
   again.

He walked to the sweet shop.

'Yes, Mrs Boffin's right,' he thought. 'There's the
   slot machine.'

'That's funny,' he thought, 'I didn't notice it a
   few minutes ago.

It's full of chocolate, too. Lovely chocolate.'

Professor Boffin put his hand in his pocket
   and took out some change.

Then he put a coin into the machine.

He waited for a bar of chocolate,

but *nothing happened.*

'This is a silly machine,' Professor Boffin said
   crossly.

He put his hand into his pocket and found another
   coin.

Then he put it into the machine.

He waited for a bar of chocolate,

but nothing happened.

Professor Boffin hit the machine hard,

but nothing happened.

Just then, a policeman came.

He heard the noise and saw Professor Boffin.

'Now, now,' the policeman said. 'What are you
   doing?'

'I put a coin into this machine a minute ago, but

I can't get any chocolate,' Professor Boffin said.

'How much did you put in?' the policeman asked.

'Two five pence pieces,' Professor Boffin said.

'Have you had a bar of chocolate yet?' the policeman asked.

'No,' Professor Boffin said crossly.

'Mm,' the policeman said. He looked at the machine.

'This is a funny machine,' he said. He hit it hard, but nothing happened.

'That's funny,' the policeman said.

He hit the machine hard again.

This time, there was a strange noise.

It sounded like little bells.

The policeman put his hand in the machine and took out two coins.

'Who put these coins into the machine?' the policeman asked.

'I did,' Professor Boffin answered.

'Well, look at them!' the policeman said.

'This one is five pence, but this thing isn't a coin. It's a button. You put the button into the machine and broke it.'

Professor Boffin remembered Mrs Boffin's button box.

'Oh dear,' he said. 'I was very careless.'

'Put in the five pence,' the policeman said.

This time a bar of chocolate came out at once.

'Thanks,' Professor Boffin said,

'now my wife can have her bar of chocolate.'

Gossip, Gossip, Gossip!

'May I speak to the Chief Inspector please?' a voice said.

'Speaking,' the Chief Inspector answered.

The Chief Inspector listened. 'What!' he said.

'What happened, sir?' a policeman asked.

'There's been a robbery at the library.

Let's go there at once,' the Chief Inspector said.

The Chief Inspector and the policeman got into their car.

They went to the library.

'Look!' the policeman said. 'There's a light on in the library.'

They both climbed into the library

and then they saw Professor Boffin and two policemen.

'Where's the thief?' the Chief Inspector asked.

'Here,' the two policemen said.

The Chief Inspector laughed.

He knows Professor Boffin well.

'There's been a mistake,' he said.

'This man isn't a thief.

This is Professor Boffin, the famous scientist.'

The next morning, *everyone heard the news*.

Mrs Mopp was at the butcher's.

She wanted to buy some meat.

Then Mrs Goff came into the butcher's.

She wanted to buy some meat, too.

Mrs Mopp spoke to her.

'Have you heard the news?' Mrs Mopp asked.

'There's been a robbery at the library.

Last night, a thief climbed into the library and *stole* some books,

but a policeman *caught* him.'

'Really!' Mrs Goff cried.

Mrs Goff bought some meat and then hurried to the baker's.

Mrs Briggs was at the baker's.

She wanted to buy some bread.

Mrs Goff spoke to her.

'Oh, Mrs Briggs,' she said. 'Have you heard the news?'

'What news?' Mrs Briggs asked.

'There's been a robbery at the library,' Mrs Goff said.

'Last night two thieves climbed into the library and stole a hundred books, but three policemen caught them.'

'Really!' Mrs Briggs said.

Mrs Briggs bought some bread and then she went to the market.

She saw Mrs Hill at the market.

Mrs Hill wanted to buy some fruit and vegetables.

'Oh, Mrs Hill,' Mrs Briggs said.

'Have you heard the news?

There's been a robbery at the library.

Last night five thieves climbed into the library and stole a thousand books.'

'A thousand books!' Mrs Hill cried.

'Yes,' Mrs Briggs answered,

'but eight policemen caught them.

The thieves are in prison now.'

'Really!' Mrs Hill said.

Mrs Hill bought some fruit and vegetables and hurried to the stationer's.

Mrs Gasbag was at the stationer's.

She wanted to buy some ink and paper.

Mrs Hill spoke to her.

'Have you heard the news?' Mrs Hill said.

'There's been a robbery at the library.

Twenty thieves climbed into the library last night and stole thousands and thousands of books.

'Really!' Mrs Gasbag said.

'Yes,' Mrs Hill answered, 'but the police caught them.'

Mrs Gasbag went home.

On the way home she met Mrs Boffin.

'Oh, Mrs Boffin,' she cried.

'Have you heard the news?

Last night fifty thieves stole all the books from the library,

but the police caught them.'

Mrs Boffin laughed.

'That's a silly story,' she said.

'Professor Boffin was at the library last night.

He didn't come home. He forgot!

Some policemen *thought he was a thief*.

They made a mistake.'

'And where's Professor Boffin now?' Mrs Gasbag asked.

'Is he in prison?'

'No,' Mrs Boffin laughed.

'He's still at the library.

He's still reading. He hasn't come home yet!'

Sandy and Billy Play a Trick

'Mum!' Sandy called. 'Billy's just come.
Can we both play in the street?'

'I don't know,' mother answered.

'Have you done your homework yet?'

'Yes.' Sandy answered. 'I've already done my homework.

I did my homework at four o'clock.'

'All right, then,' mother said.

'Go and play with Billy.'

'What can we play, Billy?' Sandy asked.

'Why don't we play that trick
with a piece of paper and a brick?' Billy asked.

'We can put a brick in a piece of paper and make a parcel.

Then we can put the parcel on the ground.'

'But we've already played that trick,' Sandy said.

'It doesn't matter,' Billy answered.

'Bring some paper, Sandy.'

Then Sandy and Billy went into the garden.

'I've just found a nice brick,' Billy said.

'What about the paper, Sandy?'

'I've already brought some paper,' Sandy said.

'And what about some string?'

'I've already brought some string as well,' Sandy said.

The boys worked very hard and made a very nice parcel.

'That looks nice,' Billy said.

'Now let's put it in the street.

We can hide behind the fence and watch.'

Sandy and Billy put the parcel in the street.

Then they went behind the fence and waited.

They waited and waited, but *no one* came.

'I'm tired,' Sandy said. 'This isn't a very good trick.'

'No one has come yet.'

'Sh!' Billy said. 'There's a man coming down the street.'

The man walked very quickly.

The boys watched him.

'He hasn't seen the parcel yet,' Billy said.

The man didn't look down at all.

He came near the parcel and kicked it with his foot.

'Ouch! My foot!' he cried.

But he still didn't look down and he didn't see the parcel.

He was in a hurry.

'He didn't see it,' Billy said sadly.

'It doesn't matter,' Sandy answered, 'because Mrs Gasbag's coming.

She's with her friend, Mrs Goff.

Let's watch them.'

'Look!' Mrs Goff said.

'What's that over there?'

'What?' Mrs Gasbag asked.

'That!' Mrs Goff said. 'It looks like a parcel.'

Mrs Gasbag and Mrs Goff came near.

'It is a parcel,' Mrs Gasbag said.

'Pick it up,' Mrs Goff said.

Mrs Gasbag picked up the parcel.

'It's terribly heavy,' she said.

'Whose is it?'

'I don't know,' Mrs Goff said.

'I can't see a name and address on it.

We must take it to the police station.'

'Let's open it first,' Mrs Gasbag said.

'Perhaps there's *something nice* in it.

Perhaps it's full of money.'

Billy and Sandy were still behind the fence.

They watched the two ladies.

Billy laughed loudly.

'Sh!' Sandy said. 'Don't laugh, Billy.'

'I can't stop,' Billy said. He laughed and laughed.

Mrs Goff and Mrs Gasbag heard him.

'What's that?' Mrs Gasbag said.

'Look!' Mrs Goff cried. 'It's Billy Briggs and Sandy Clark.

They're behind the fence. They're laughing.'

'Hullo, Billy. Hullo, Sandy.' Mrs Gasbag said.

'We've just found this parcel.

We found it a moment ago.

Is this your parcel, Billy?'

'No,' Billy said.

'Let's open it,' Mrs Gasbag said.

She opened the parcel and found the brick.

'Oh, look! It's a brick,' she said crossly.

Billy and Sandy laughed.

Mrs Goff laughed, too.

'We played a trick on you,' Billy said.

'That was a funny trick,' Mrs Goff said.

But Mrs Gasbag was cross.

'Don't do it again!' she said.

Professor Boffin Goes to London

'What are you going to do tomorrow, dear?' Mrs Boffin asked.

'Let me see,' Professor Boffin answered.

He thought about it for a few minutes.

'Ah yes,' he said. 'I shall go to London tomorrow.

I shall catch the train at eight o'clock.'

'When'll you come home?' Mrs Boffin asked.

'I'll be home at about four o'clock in the afternoon.'

The next day, Professor Boffin went to London.

He went and saw his old friend, Professor Pottle.

Professor Boffin told Professor Pottle about his robot.

'That's very interesting,' Professor Pottle said.

They had lunch together and they talked and talked.

'My robot's name is "Robert" ', Professor Boffin said.

'He helps Mrs Boffin a lot.

He's very nice too, but he's sometimes naughty.

He's just like a child sometimes.'

'Can he talk?' Professor Pottle asked.

'No, he can't talk, but he understands English very well.'

They both talked for a long time.

Suddenly, Professor Boffin looked at his watch.

'My goodness!' he cried. 'It's nearly three o'clock.

I must leave now.

I have been here for six hours.

I've been here since nine o'clock.

I must catch my train.'

Professor Boffin said goodbye to Professor Pottle.

'Goodbye, Professor Pottle,' he said.

'I'll see you in a few weeks' time.'

'Goodbye,' Professor Pottle answered.

Professor Boffin hurried to the station.

He bought a newspaper and then he bought a ticket.

He got on the train.

'I'll read my newspaper on the train,' he thought.

Soon the train went out of the station.

Professor Boffin read his newspaper.

He read it for a long time

and he felt very sleepy.

'I feel very sleepy,' he thought.

'I'll go to bed early tonight.

Mrs Boffin will have a nice hot meal for me.

I'll have my dinner early and then I'll have a bath and go to bed.

That'll be nice,' he thought

He shut his eyes and thought about it,

and soon he was fast asleep.

The train stopped at lots of stations,

but Professor Boffin didn't wake up.

He was fast asleep.

Suddenly he heard a voice. 'Come on, sir,' a man said.

'You can't sleep on this train.'

'Wh . . . What?' Professor Boffin cried.

'You've been asleep,' the man said. 'You can't sleep here.'

'Where are we?' Professor Boffin asked.

'We're at the seaside,' the man said.

'The train stops here.'

'At the seaside!' Professor Boffin cried.

'But I must get off at Scrimpton.'

'Scrimpton!' the man said. 'We passed Scrimpton hours ago.'

Professor Boffin looked at his watch.

It was five past eight.

'Oh dear!' he said.

'I must catch a train back to Scrimpton.'

'And you must buy another ticket,' the man said.

Professor Boffin bought another ticket.

He paid a lot of money.

The seaside is a long way from Scrimpton.

Then he caught the next train home.

He arrived home at midnight.

Mrs Boffin was asleep, but she woke up.

She went downstairs.

'You're very late, dear,' she said.

'I've been to the seaside,' Professor Boffin said.

'Didn't you go to London?' Mrs Boffin asked.

'Oh yes,' he said.

Then he told her about the train.

'You must go to bed,' Mrs Boffin said. 'You're very tired.'

'No, I'm not,' Professor Boffin said.

'I had a nice long sleep on the train. I'm not tired now,

but I'm very hungry. Can I have my dinner please?'

'Your dinner!' Mrs Boffin cried. 'It's nearly time for breakfast!'

From Sue's Diary: My Cat Ginger

I've got a lovely cat. Her name's Ginger.

Three months ago, Ginger had five *kittens*.

We gave a kitten to Billy and a kitten to Tom.

We gave a kitten to Liz and a kitten to Lillie.

We *kept* one of the kittens.

He's a very sweet little kitten,

but he's often very naughty.

Yesterday, he climbed the big tree in our garden.

Sandy and I were at school.

We came home from school at four o'clock.

I played with Ginger after tea, but where was our kitten?

I asked mum. 'Have you seen our little kitten, mum?' I asked.

'No,' mum said. 'Perhaps he's in the garden.'

Sandy and I went into the garden.

We looked *everywhere*.

'That's funny,' Sandy said. 'He's not here.'

Suddenly, I heard a soft 'meow'!

'Listen!' I cried. We looked round the garden again,

but the kitten wasn't there.

'Look!' Sandy said. 'He's up there!'

I looked up. Sandy was right.

The little kitten was high up in the tree.

'He can't get down,' I said. 'He's afraid.'

'What'll we do?' Sandy asked.

'Can you climb up there, Sandy?' I asked.

Sandy looked up. 'No, it's terribly high,' he said.

'Those *branches* aren't very strong.'

'I know,' I said. 'We'll get Ginger.

Ginger'll climb up the tree and bring down the kitten.'

I ran into the house and got Ginger.

I brought Ginger into the garden and showed the kitten to her.

Ginger's very clever. She understood at once.

She climbed the tree quickly.

'She'll bring the kitten down,' I said.

Sandy and I looked up. 'She's very high up now,' Sandy said,

'but she can't reach the kitten.'

Ginger tried to reach the kitten. She tried again

and again.

'Meow! Meow!' she said. She was afraid.

Then she tried to climb down.

'She can't climb down!' I cried.

'Now Ginger and her baby kitten are up the tree.'

'Oh, what'll we do?' Sandy asked.

'Let's ask dad,' I said.

Dad came into the garden and looked up the tree.

'Our ladder isn't very big,' he said.

'We can't reach Ginger and her kitten with our
  ladder.'

'What'll we do then, dad?' I asked.

'We can't let Ginger and the kitten stay up the tree.
  They'll *fall*.'

'Then we must call the *fire-brigade*,' dad said.

Dad telephoned the fire-brigade and told them
about Ginger and the little kitten.

Soon a big red *fire-engine* arrived at our house.

Four firemen carried a very long ladder into our
  garden.

They put the ladder *against* the tree.

Sandy and I watched them.

'They'll soon reach her,' Sandy said.

'Look! The fireman's very near.'

'I can't reach them,' the fireman called.

'I must climb on to the tree.'

'Be careful!' father called. 'Those branches aren't
  very strong.'

The fireman climbed on to the branches and got
  Ginger.

Soon he got the kitten, too.

'Hey!' the fireman called.

'I've got Ginger and her kitten, but I can't get
  down now.'

'Oh dear!' father said. 'What'll we do now?'

Father looked at the other three firemen.

'It's all right,' one of them said.

'We'll move the ladder a little.'

They moved the ladder and the fireman reached
  it.

Then he climbed down very quickly.

'There you are,' he said to me.

'Thank you very much,' I said.

I took Ginger and the kitten into the house and mother made some nice strong tea for the firemen.

The End of Term

It was the end of term. It was the last day of school. Sandy, Sue and their friends were very happy.

Their teachers gave the children their reports and said goodbye.

'Have a good holiday!' the teachers said.

Sandy and Sue went home. They took their reports with them.

Sandy looked sad. 'My report's never very good,' he said.

'You're lucky, Sue. You always have a good report.'

The children arrived home and Sue gave her report to father.

Father read it carefully.

'Mm,' father said. '"English, very good. French, very good.

Sue works very well."'

Father smiled. 'Nice work, Sue,' he said.

'This is a very good report.'

Then he looked at Sandy.

'What about yours, Sandy?'

'Here's mine,' Sandy said. He gave his report to father.

'Sandy!' father cried. 'It says: "Very good work."

That's unusual for you, Sandy!'

Then father looked again. 'Just a minute,' he said.

'They've made a mistake.

This report doesn't belong to you.'

'Who does it belong to?' Sandy asked.

'It belongs to your friend, Simon,' father said.

'You've got his report and he's got yours.'

'Poor Simon!' Sandy said.

'Simon always works hard. He's always well-behaved
and he always gets good reports.'
'Will you go to Simon's house please,' father said,
'and give him his report.'
'Shall I take my report from Simon?' Sandy asked.
'Of course!' father said.

What's happening at Simon's house? Let's see.
Simon has just come home from school, too.
He has given his report to his father.
'Mm,' Simon's father said. 'This isn't a very good report, Simon.
Your teacher says: "He doesn't work hard and he's sometimes lazy!"'
Simon's face was red.
'Oh, dear,' Simon said. 'That's not a very good report.'
Simon's father looked at the report again.
'Just a minute!' he cried. 'This report isn't yours.
It belongs to Sandy Clark.
They've made a mistake at school.'
Simon smiled. Just then, the door-bell rang.
It was Sandy. 'I've brought Simon's report,' Sandy said.
'They made a mistake at school this afternoon.
They gave me Simon's report and gave my report to Simon.'
'I know,' Simon said. 'Here's your report, Sandy.'
Sandy took his report and read it.
'My dad won't like this,' he said.
Poor Sandy! He didn't feel very well.
He went home and gave his report to his father.
Sandy's father read it carefully.
'"He doesn't work very hard and he's sometimes lazy."
Mm,' father said. 'That's not very good.'
Then father looked at the report again.
'Just a minute,' he said. 'I haven't read it all.
It says: "He doesn't work very hard and he's

61

sometimes lazy,
but this year, his work has been good."'
Sandy smiled. 'I didn't see that,' he said.
'That's nice, Sandy,' father said. 'You see, your
report isn't bad at all. Now you can both have
a nice holiday.
How long'll your holiday last?'
'It'll last for eight weeks,' Sandy said.
'Eight weeks!' father cried. 'You're very lucky.
My holiday doesn't last for eight weeks.'
'What are we going to do during the holidays?'
Sandy asked.
'We'll go to the seaside,' father said.
'We'll spend four weeks at the seaside.
We'll go next week.
And this evening, you can both have a lovely treat.
We can all go to a restaurant and have a nice meal.'
'Oh, thanks, dad!' the children cried.
'We're going to have a lovely treat today,' Sandy
cried.
Then Sue said, 'We're going to have a lovely
holiday, too!'

The Holidays

Sandy and Sue had a good time during the
summer holidays. They left home on August 15th.
They stayed at an *hotel* near the sea. It was a
lovely little hotel and the children enjoyed their
holiday. The name of the hotel was 'Seaview'. It
was in a beautiful *bay*. The name of the bay was
'Long Bay'.

Father, mother, Sandy and Sue went to the
beach every day. They can all swim very well.
Sue can dive, too, but Sandy can't dive. He
always jumps into the water.

One day, Sue said to Sandy, "You mustn't
jump into the water, Sandy. You must dive."

"I can't dive," Sandy said.

"Watch me," Sue said. "It's easy. Look. Like
this." Sue dived into the water beautifully and

Sandy watched her. "Now you do it, Sandy," Sue called.

Sandy put his arms over his head and dived. "Ouch!" he shouted.

"What's the matter?" Sue asked and she laughed.

"I hit my *tummy* on the water," Sandy said. "It's not funny."

"It was very funny," Sue said. "Do it again, Sandy."

Sandy went out of the water and dived again. "You're right, Sue," he said. "It's easy."

"Mum, dad!" Sue called. "Watch Sandy. He can dive now."

Mother and father watched Sandy. He dived into the water again. He dived very well. "That's very good," mother and father said. Then mother and father dived into the water, too.

Sandy went to the beach and got his *snorkel*. Mother, father and Sue didn't see him. Sandy put on his snorkel and went back into the water. Sandy can swim under water very well and he swam *towards* Sue. Then he dived under Sue and *pinched* her toes.

"Ouch!" Sue cried.

"What's the matter?" mother asked.

"There's a big fish under the water," Sue said. "It pinched my toes."

"Don't be silly, Sue," mother said. "There aren't any big fish here. Mother, father and Sue didn't see Sandy. Sandy dived under mother and pinched her toes, too. "Ouch!" mother cried.

"What's the matter, Betty?" father asked.

"Sue's right, Jim," mother said. "There's a big fish under the water. It pinched my toes, too."

"I'll have a look under the water," father said. Father can swim very well. He dived down and swam under the water. Of course, he saw Sandy. But Sandy didn't see his father. Sandy swam towards Sue. He wanted to pinch his sister again.

Then father swam behind him and *grabbed* his foot. He pulled Sandy out of the water. Father laughed and Sandy laughed, too. "You're right, Betty," he said. "There is a big fish in the water. I've just caught it."

"Where is it?" Sue and mother asked.

"Here," father said and he *pointed* at Sandy.

"Sandy can swim like a fish and he can dive like a *seagull*," father said.

"Yes," Sue said, "and he can pinch like a *crab!*"

Sandy and Sue have gone back to school now, but they often remember their summer holidays. Don't you?

The Blakes Move In

"Where have you been, children?" Mother asked.

"We've been next door, mum," Sue answered.

"Next door?" mother asked. "Where? To Mrs Gasbag's?"

"No, mum. To the *other* house," Sandy said.

"But that house is empty," mother said.

"No, it isn't, mum. Some new neighbours have arrived." Sue said. "Look out of the window. That's Mr Blake. And that's his wife. They've got three children: Alan, Wendy and Timmy."

"How do you know their names?" mother asked.

"We've already met them, mum." Sue answered.

Mother looked out of the window again. "Who are those two men?" she asked.

"They're workmen, mum," Sandy said. "Their names are Dick and Harry. They're very strong. They're carrying a piano."

Dick and Harry carried the piano into the house. They put it in the kitchen. Then they carried it to another room. Mrs Blake came in and looked at it. "My goodness!" she cried. "You've turned it upside-down!"

64

"Sorry, Mrs," Dick and Harry said.

"Bring that heavy table in now," Mrs Blake said. "It's going to rain. You can turn the piano over in a moment."

Dick and Harry went out to the van. The heavy table was in the street near the van. The two workmen carried it into the house. "Careful, Dick," Harry said. "Don't drop it on your toes." Suddenly, they heard a noise. *Bang! Crash!*

"What's that?" Harry asked.

"I don't know," Dick said. "Put the table down, Harry." They put the table down. Then Mrs Blake hurried downstairs.

"What's that noise?" she asked.

"We don't know, Mrs," Dick said.

"Have you brought the bathroom mirror in yet?" Mrs Blake asked.

"Yes," Harry said.

"When did you bring it in?" Mrs Blake asked.

"We brought it in a moment ago, Mrs," Harry said.

"Where did you put it?" Mrs Blake asked.

"On the floor, Mrs," Harry said.

"Which floor?" Mrs Blake asked.

"This floor, Mrs," Harry said.

Dick looked on the floor.

"Eh! Harry!" he cried. "Harry! The mirror! Look! You're standing on it."

"Oh! Oh! My beautiful mirror," Mrs Blake cried.

"Sorry, Mrs," Harry said.

"You broke it with your big feet," Mrs Blake said. "You're a careless man!"

"Sorry, Mrs," Harry said.

"I'll pick up the pieces," Dick said. He picked up the pieces. "Ouch!" he cried.

"What's the matter, Dick?" Harry asked.

"Look!" Dick cried. "I've just cut my finger. It's *bleeding*."

"Oh! Oh!" Mrs Blake cried. "Now there's

blood on my nice clean *carpet*. Get out of the house, both of you!"

The two workmen ran out of the house. "We can bring in some chairs," they said.

Just then, Mr Blake arrived. He was in a hurry.

"Where have you been, dear?" Mrs Blake asked.

"I've been in the living-room," Mr Blake said. "Have you seen my new hat, dear?"

"No, I haven't seen your new hat," Mrs Blake said. "Where did you put it?"

"I put it in the living-room. It was there a moment ago, but it isn't there now. It's a very good hat. It cost a lot of money."

"Well I haven't seen it," Mrs Blake said. She was cross. Then Dick and Harry came in. They had some chairs.

"Put those chairs down and go into the living-room," Mrs Blake said. "Turn the piano over. It's upside-down."

Dick and Harry went into the living-room. They are very strong men and they turned the piano over quickly.

"What's that, Harry?" Dick asked.

"I don't know," Harry said. "It was under the piano."

Then Mr Blake came into the room. "Oh! Oh! Oh!" he cried. "It's my hat. My lovely new hat. Look at it now!"

Father Meets the Blakes

Father was in the garden with the children. He cut the *grass* and the children helped him. "Have you met our new neighbours yet, dad?" Sandy asked.

"No, I haven't, Sandy," father said.

"Their name is Blake," Sue said. "They have three children. There are two boys. Their names are Alan and Timmy. There is one girl. Her name is Wendy."

Then Mr Blake went into his garden and the children noticed him. "Look, dad," Sandy said. "There's Mr Blake."

Mr Blake looked over the fence and smiled at father and the children. "Good afternoon," he said.

Father smiled at Mr Blake. "Good afternoon," he answered.

"My name's George Blake," Mr Blake said.

"My name's Jim Clark," father said.

Mr Blake looked at father's garden. "You have a lovely garden," he said. Then he looked at his own garden. "Look at my garden," he said. "It isn't a garden at all. I must work very hard and I'm not a good *gardener*." Poor Mr Blake! His garden was full of *weeds*. "Excuse me, Mr Clark," he said. "May I call you Jim?"

"Of course, you may," father said. "Can I call you George?"

"Certainly," Mr Blake said. "We are neighbours now. It's so good to have neighbours."

"Yes," father said.

Mr Blake watched father. Father cut the grass and the children helped him. "Jim," he called.

"Yes," father answered and he stopped work again.

"I haven't got many *garden tools*. May I *borrow* you *spade* and your *garden fork* please?

"Of course, you may," father said. "I'll get them for you." Father got the spade and fork for Mr Blake and gave them to him.

Just then, Mrs Blake came into the garden. "Good afternoon," she said to father. "My name's Marion Blake."

"I'm Jim Clark," father said and smiled. "Please call me Jim."

"And you must call me Marion," Mrs Blake said. "It's so nice to have neighbours. This house has been empty for a long time. We must do a

67

lot of work. May I borrow your ladder please?"

"Of course," father said. "I'll get it for you."
Father got the ladder. "Here you are, Marion,"
he said.

The ladder was very heavy. "Please let me
help you." father said and he carried the ladder
into Mrs Blake's house. Then he went into Mr
Blake's garden.

"This is hard work, Jim," Mr Blake said
"I'm a very bad gardener."

"Please let me help you," father said.

"Thank you very much, Jim," Mr Blake said.
"Perhaps you can *dig* the garden for me."

"All right, George," father said.

Mother was in the kitchen. She looked out of
the window, but father wasn't in the garden. So
she called Sandy, "Sandy," she said. "Tell your
father to bring the ladder into the kitchen please.
I want him to fix this shelf."

"He can't, mum," Sandy said. "Mrs Blake has
borrowed our ladder."

"It doesn't matter," mother said. "I'll come
into the garden and help your father." Mother
went into the garden, but, of course, father
wasn't there.

Just then, Mrs Blake looked over the fence.
"Hullo, Betty," she said. "May I borrow some
flour and some sugar please?"

"Of course, Marion," mother said. "I'll get
some for you." Mother went to the kitchen and
got some flour and some sugar. "Have you seen
Jim?" she asked Mrs Blake.

Mrs Blake laughed. "We've borrowed your
spade, your garden fork, your ladder, some flour
and some sugar. And we've borrowed your
husband, too. He's in our garden. He's helping
George. It's so nice to have neighbours!"

The Wrong Car Yesterday father saw Mr Blake. He told him about his car.

"Betty tried to unlock the door of this car," father said, "but she couldn't. Do you know why? It was the wrong car. It wasn't our car. It didn't belong to us. Then a stranger ran up to us and said, 'What are you doing to my car?'"

Mr Blake laughed. "That happened to me, too," he answered. "Let me tell you the story."

"Please tell me the story," father said.

"Well," Mr Blake began. "One day last year I went shopping with my wife. Marion always buys lots of things at the shops. She bought a dress and then she said to me, 'Would you carry this dress for me, George?' and she gave it to me. She bought a big hat and then she said to me, 'Could you carry this hat for me please, George?' and she gave it to me. She bought a blouse and then she said to me, 'Could you carry this blouse for me please, George?' She bought lots of things and I carried them. I had lots of parcels. My hands were full. I couldn't see, so I wasn't able to walk properly. 'Please show me the way, Marion,' I said. 'I can't see.' Marion showed me the way and we went back to the car together. Marion stopped in front of a small red car.

'This car is ours,' she said.

'I'll open the door, dear,' I said. I put my hand in my pocket and found my key. I took the key out of my pocket and put it in the lock. Then I tried to unlock the door of the car. "That's funny," I said to Marion.

'What's funny, dear?' she asked.

'The key fits into the lock,' I said, 'but it won't turn.' I tried to turn the key, but I couldn't. I wasn't able to turn it at all. I tried very hard and suddenly, the key broke. I was very cross. I said some very bad things. I dropped all the parcels.

'Be careful,' Marion said. 'Be careful of my new clothes.'

'I don't care about your new clothes,' I said. 'I can't get into my car. I've broken my key.' I was terribly terribly cross. So I broke the window of the car and opened the door. 'Put the parcels in the back seat,' I said. 'Now get into the car please.'

Just then a man ran up to us. He was very cross, too. 'I saw you,' he shouted. 'I saw you. You broke the window of my car.'

'This is my car,' I said. 'My key broke in the lock and I broke the window.'

'It isn't your car!' the man shouted. 'You're a thief!' 'It's my car. Police! Police!' he called.

A policeman heard him and came to the car. 'Now, now,' the policeman said. 'What's happening here?'

'This man and this woman are thieves,' the man cried. 'They're taking my car.'

'Is this your car?' the policeman asked the man.

'Yes,' the man said and he showed the policeman some papers.

'Mm,' the policeman said. Then he looked at me and I looked at him.

'I'm sorry,' I said. 'I've made a mistake. My car is exactly like this one. I had a lot of parcels in my hands and I couldn't see properly.'

'Mm,' the policeman said. 'I often hear this story. Will you come to the police station with me?'

We went to the station and at last the police *believed* me. I paid a lot of money to the other man. Then my wife and I walked home and I carried all those parcels."

"Why?" father asked. "Couldn't you find your car?"

"Yes," Mr Blake said. "We were able to find our car, but of course, we didn't have a key!"

"That's a funny story," father said and he laughed and laughed.

At the Circus

Last week father took the children to the circus. They saw lots of things, but they liked the clown best. The clown played many clever tricks. The clown appeared with the weight-lifter. The clown's name was Boris. The weight-lifter's name was Marvo.

Marvo was a very strong man. There was a heavy weight on the *ground,* but Marvo was strong enough to lift it. The weight was easy for him to lift.

Then Boris appeared. He looked very funny. He wore a funny hat and he had a big red nose. His shoes were very big.

"His shoes are like boats," Sandy said.

Poor Boris! He couldn't walk easily because his shoes were so big. He walked like this: *flip, flop,* flip, flop. And he often *fell over.* Suddenly Boris saw Marvo, the weight-lifter, and laughed. Then he tried to lift Marvo's big weight. He tried and tried, but it was too difficult for him to lift it. He wasn't able to lift it at all. Marvo watched Boris, then he pushed him away and lifted up the weight. Boris fell over and hurt his head.

Then Boris found his own 'weight'. It wasn't a *real* weight. It was just a bar and two balloons. Boris *pretended that* his weight was very heavy. He tried to lift it and he pretended that he couldn't. Marvo watched him. Then Boris picked up the weight with one hand and held it above his head. He showed it to Marvo. Marvo was very *surprised.* Suddenly, Boris hit Marvo on the head with one of the balloons. Of course, this didn't hurt Marvo at all, but he pretended that the clown hurt him.

Marvo ran after Boris. Boris tried to run, but he couldn't. He wasn't able to run because his shoes were so big. Marvo caught Boris and took the weight. Then he burst the balloons and broke the bar with his hands. Boris watched this, then he took out his *handkerchief* and cried. Marvo *felt sorry* for Boris. He went near him and suddenly Boris gave him a hard kick in the leg. Marvo pretended that he couldn't walk. His leg hurt, so it was difficult for him to walk. He was very, very cross. He caught Boris again and he took off one of Boris's shoes. Then he put Boris over his knees and *spanked* him with the shoe. Boris cried like a baby: *Boo hoo!* Boo hoo! He took out his handkerchief again and cried and cried.

Marvo didn't pay any attention to Boris. He went back to his weight and lifted it up. What did Boris do? Well, he went away and came back with a *bucket*. He stood behind Marvo and Marvo couldn't see him. Suddenly, Boris put the bucket over Marvo's head. Marvo dropped the weight and shouted. He ran here and there, but he couldn't see at all. He wasn't able to see because the bucket was over his eyes. Boris picked up a small weight and hit the bucket very hard. Marvo tried to pull the bucket off, but he wasn't able to. He looked very funny with the bucket on his head. Boris laughed and laughed and the children *clapped*. Sandy and Sue enjoyed the programme very much. Have you ever been to a circus? Didn't you enjoy it, too?

The Dancing Competition It was a very *important* day yesterday. Sue *entered a dancing competition*. There were lots of girls in the competition. Mother, father and Sandy went to see the competition. *"Good luck, Sue!"* they said.

Sue wore a pretty white dress and lovely *silver* shoes. She wore a number on her back. Her number was 16. There were twenty girls in the competition. They danced together and six *judges* watched them. Then the dancing ended and the judges talked about the dancers.

"I think numbers 6, 16, 7 and 8 were very good indeed," a judge said. "They were the best."

"I *agree*," another judge said. "Numbers 2, 4, 9 and 12 were very bad indeed. The· ·. · the worst."

The *judges* agreed about the best dancers and the worst dancers, but they couldn't agree about the *winners*. They talked and talked.

"Number 7 was better than number 8," one of the judges said.

"I don't agree," another judge said. "Number 7 is a taller girl than number 8. She dances very well, but she is not as good as number 8."

"Who was that girl on the left?" one of the judges said. "She danced very well."

"That was number 6," another judge said.

"Number 16 was the quickest and neatest of them all," another judge said.

"I don't agree. She's a good dancer, but she's not the quickest and the neatest."

"I don't agree," another judge said. "She was very good indeed."

The judges talked and talked. At last they appeared and all the people waited to hear them. The girls stood behind the judges. They looked very pretty. They all wore white dresses and silver shoes. Which girl was the prettiest? That's a very hard question. They were all so pretty.

Sue could see her mother and father and Sandy. Sue smiled at them and mother, father and Sandy smiled at Sue.

"Will she win, Jim?" mother asked father.

"I don't know, Betty," father said. "She danced very well. She danced better than numbers 2 and 9."

"Numbers 2 and 9!" mother cried. "They didn't dance well at all. They were awful. Their dancing was very poor."

"Quiet please," the judges called.

"Sh!" father said. "They're going to call the

winners. They always give the third prize first, then the second and then the first."

One of the judges stood up. "It was very difficult for us to judge this competition," he said. "All the girls danced so well. They are all very good dancers indeed. The third prize went to number 8. Number 8 came third."

The people *clapped* and number 8 went to the judges. She *shook hands* with them and she got £2 and a *certificate*.

'The next prize went to number 6," the judge said. "Number 6 came second."

Number 6 went to the judges and shook hands. She got a prize of £5 and a certificate.

"And the first prize . . ." the judge went on.

"Oh!" mother said.

"The first prize," the judge said, "went to number 16!"

Mother and father and Sandy clapped and clapped.

"Hurray!" Sandy shouted. "Good old Sue!"

Sue went to the judges and they gave her a *silver cup* and a prize of £10. Sue was very happy.

"Congratulations," mother, father and Sandy said.

"It's the happiest day of my life," Sue said.

"Let's see the cup," Sandy said. "What are you going to do with it?"

"I'm going to put it on a shelf in my room," Sue said.

"But first I'm going to fill it with *champagne,"* father said, "and we can all drink from it. We're all very *proud* of you Sue."

Mr Blake's Car

Mr Blake's car is very old indeed. It's a very old car, so it isn't very reliable. Of course, Mr Blake doesn't *think* so. He loves his car. "My car is the smallest car in the world. But it's the most reliable and the most well-behaved car I've ever seen," he always says. "Of course, it's less expensive than a big car. Still, it's as good as a big car."

Last week, Mr Blake took his family out. Mr and Mrs Blake sat in the front of the car and the children sat in the back.

"We can have a picnic today," Mr Blake said. "But first we must go to the *garage.*" Mr Blake drove to the garage.

"Have you got enough *petrol?*" the man at the garage asked.

"No," Mr Blake answered. "Will you fill the car please?"

"You haven't got enough *air* in your tyres," the man said. "You need some more. Shall I blow them up for you?"

"Yes, please," Mr Blake said, so the man blew up the tyres.

"Do you need any *oil?*" the man said.

Mr Blake looked at the oil in the engine. "No," he said. "I've got plenty of oil. There's enough oil in the engine." Mr Blake paid the man and drove away.

"Where shall we go, dear?" Mrs Blake asked.

"I don't know," Mr Blake said.

"Let's go to the seaside," the children said.

"All right," Mr Blake said, "but it's rather cold at this time of the year. Still, we can spend the day at the seaside."

It was rather cold, but the Blakes had a lovely day. They played games on the *beach.* They ate their sandwiches on the beach, too. They were very hungry.

"Let's see," Alan said. "Who can eat the most sandwiches? Let's have a *competition.*"

Alan, Wendy and Timmy had a competition. Alan had seven sandwiches, but Wendy won. She had seven and a half.

"Oh, I can't eat any more," Alan said.

Later they all got into the car and Mr Blake

started the engine. The car went very well, but suddenly it stopped. They were *a long way from home*. "What's the matter, dear?" Mrs Blake asked.

"I don't know," Mr Blake said. "I'll have a look at the engine." He got out of the car and had a look.

"Can you see anything?" the children asked.

"No," Mr Blake said. "I can't understand it."

"The most reliable car in the world," Alan said and laughed.

Mr Blake tried to start the engine. He turned the key, but he couldn't start it. "Perhaps there's too little petrol," he wife said.

"No, there isn't," Mr Blake said. "We filled it this morning. Get out and push. We can all push," he said.

All the family got out and Mr Blake sat in front. The family pushed. The car was very small so it was easy for them to push it. They pushed and pushed, but it didn't start.

"What shall we do?" Mrs Blake said. "It's rather late."

Just then, a big truck stopped near them. "Do you want any help?" the driver asked.

"Yes, please," Mr Blake said. "My engine won't start."

"I'll pull your car," the truck driver said. He got out of his truck. "Oh dear," he said. "I can't find a *rope* or a *chain*."

"What shall we do now?" Mrs Blake said.

"Don't worry," the truck driver said.

There were two workmen in the truck and the driver called them. "You can help us too," he said to the Blakes. "We're going to lift your car on to the back of the truck. We'll carry you home."

It was easy to lift the little car. The Blakes sat in their own car and the driver took them home.

"Thank you very much." Mr Blake said.

"It's all right," the driver said.

"You see," Mr Blake said later. "Our car *broke down,* but it's still the most reliable car in the world. It took us to the seaside and it brought us home, too."

Gramophone Records

Last month father bought a new record-player. Now he wants to buy lots of new gramophone records. He goes to the record shop very often. Father likes *classical* music very much, so he buys lots of classical records. He went to the record shop yesterday. He saw some very nice records there.

"I haven't got these two records," he said to an assistant.

"They're both very good records," the assistant answered.

"Are they the same quality?" father asked.

"No, they are different in quality," the assistant said. "The record on the left is better than the record on the right. Of course, the record on the left is more expensive than the one on the right."

"I like records very much," father said, "but they're very expensive. May I have one of those please?"

"Which of the two do you want, sir?" the assistant asked.

"The cheaper one," father said.

The assistant smiled politely. She put the record in a bag. Father paid some money and left the shop. He went home quickly because he wanted to play his record. At home, father played the record on his new record-player. He called Betty.

"Come and listen to this new record dear," he said. "It's very beautiful music."

Mother listened to the new record. "Yes, dear;" she said. "It's lovely music."

Just then the children came in.

"You must listen to this new record," father said.

"It's very nice," Sue said. "We like classical music, but we like *pop,* too."

"Ugh!" father said. "Don't talk to me about pop!"

The children enjoyed the music very much. Then Sandy said, "I want to buy a record, too, but I haven't got any money. Have you got any money, Sue?"

"I've got no money," Sue said.

"Neither have I," mother said. "Don't look at me, Sandy."

"I've got none either," father said. "I've just bought this new record."

"Never mind," Sandy said. "Let's go out and play, Sue."

Sandy and Sue went out to play. Then mother spoke to father. "You can give Sandy some extra pocket-money, Jim. He likes good music. He wants to buy a record."

"Perhaps you're right," father said. Then he called Sandy and Sue. "Haven't you got any money?" he asked them.

"No, we're broke," they said.

"Well," father said. "I'm going to give you both a little present. You can go out and buy a good gramophone record."

Father gave Sandy and Sue some money and they went to the record shop. They didn't look at the classical records!

"Father's got plenty of classical records," Sue said, "but he hasn't got any pop records."

"He doesn't like pop," Sandy said.

"But we do," Sue said.

Sandy and Sue listened to two new pop records. "How much are these?" they asked the assistant.

"They're different in price," the assistant said. "The larger one is more expensive."

"May we have the cheaper one please?" Sue

said.

The children bought the record and ran home quickly. Sandy played the record on the new record-player.

"Come and listen to our new record, dad," Sandy said.

"I can here it from here," father said. "It's a terrible noise! Is it music?"

"Of course, it is," Sue said. "It's pop music."

"It sounds awful," father said. "I gave you some extra pocket-money because I wanted you to buy a good record.,

"Oh, dad!" Sue cried. "Sometimes you're so *old-fashioned!*"

Mother and Sue Go Shopping

Yesterday, mother and Sue went shopping together. "You need some new clothes, Sue," mother said. "You haven't got many dresses and you need a new pair of shoes. We can go shopping together."

"Oh thank you, mum!" Sue said. "I'm going to enjoy that."

"I shall buy some nice clothes for you," mother said.

Sue looked cross. "Mum," she said, "you always *choose* my clothes. I want to choose my own clothes."

"Well, you can help me, Sue," mother said. "I always let you choose your own clothes."

"No, you don't," Sue said. "You always choose them for me. You say: 'This suits you. That doesn't suit you. You can't wear this.' I'm a big girl now. I'm twelve years old. I can choose my own clothes."

"We'll see," mother said. "Now *get ready* please."

Mother and Sue went to the shops. They looked at the lovely window display in a big shop.

"Look at that lovely blouse, mum," Sue said.

79

"How much is it? It's £1·50 pence."

"Yes, it's a lovely blouse," mother said, "but it's not for you. It doesn't suit you. It's all right for me, but it's not for a girl like you."

Sue didn't say anything. She looked cross. Then they both went into the shop. First they bought a pair of shoes. They went to the *shoe department*.

"A pair of shoes for the young lady please," mother said.

"What size?" the assistant asked.

"Size 30," mother said.

The assistant brought a few pairs of shoes and mother let Sue choose a pair. "I like this pair," Sue said. "They're lovely red shoes and they're a nice shape."

"They're a nice price, too," mother said. "They cost £3·75 pence. They're too expensive for me. I can't afford £3·75. You must choose a cheaper pair."

Sue found a cheaper pair. They cost £2·14 pence. Then mother and Sue went to the dress department.

"I want a dress for this young lady, please," mother said.

"What size?" the assistant asked.

"I don't know," mother said.

"Then we must measure you," the assistant said to Sue. The assistant measured Sue and said. "You're quite a tall girl. You need a big dress."

Mother let Sue choose her own dress. Sue chose a lovely green and white dress. She tried it on and looked in the mirror. "Does it suit me?" she asked her mother.

"Yes," mother said. "It's the right length and it looks nice."

"I like it very much, mum," Sue said. "May I have it please?"

"Of course," mother said. "It isn't too expensive."

"You see!" Sue smiled. "I can choose my

own clothes."

Mother smiled too. "Now you need a blouse," she said.

Sue wanted the blouse in the window and mother said no.

"It doesn't suit you," mother said.

Sue *insisted* and mother insisted and they had a big *argument*.

Then mother said "All right" and she bought the blouse.

It really didn't suit Sue at all. "That blouse is for a woman of 35, not for a girl of 12," mother said.

"I don't care," Sue said. "I'm going to wear it."

Mother and Sue went home with the new things. "Thank you very much, mum," Sue said. "I want to show dad all these new things."

Mother didn't say anything. She looked at Sue and said at last, "I like your dress and I like your shoes, but I don't like that blouse!"

Sue showed her new clothes to father. Father liked the dress and shoes, but he didn't like the blouse either. "It really doesn't suit you, Sue," he said. "It looks funny."

Sue looked in the mirror. "You're right, dad," she said. "It looks very funny and I can't wear it."

"What can we do with it, Betty?" father asked.

"Well," mother said. "I like it and it's almost my size."

"Try it on," father said.

Mother tried it on and it fitted her.

"It suits you very well," Sue and father said.

Mother laughed. "I didn't choose any clothes for you, Sue," she said, "but you *chose* a blouse for me!"

Timmy Mrs Blake's little boy often says funny things. A few weeks ago, he said to his father: "Ours is the nicest garden in the neighbourhood. Nobody's grass is longer than ours." Well, yesterday at tea-time, Timmy was very, very hungry. He ate and ate and ate and he couldn't stop.

"Would you like a *boiled* egg?" his mother asked.

"Yes, please. I'd love one," Timmy said.

"Would you like some bread and butter?"

"Yes, please. I'd love some," Timmy said. "I'm very hungry."

"So am I," his sister, Wendy, said, "but I'm not as hungry as Timmy is."

Everyone finished tea, but Timmy didn't finish. "My goodness, young man," his father said, "you'll *burst*. Aren't you *full* yet?"

"No, I haven't started yet," Timmy said.

"Well, I can't eat any more," Mr Blake said.

"Neither can I," Wendy said.

"And I don't want any more," Alan said.

"Neither do I," Mrs Blake said.

"Mum," Timmy said. "Would you cut another slice of bread for me please?"

"Another slice of bread?" his mother said. "There's none on the table." His mother looked for some bread, but she couldn't find any. "I'm sorry," she said. "There's none left, Timmy. You mustn't eat any more. You'll burst. Aren't you full yet?"

"No," Timmy said. "I haven't started yet."

Wendy laughed. "You'll get fat," she said. "There's a boy at school. His name's Billy Briggs. He's terribly fat. You'll be like him. He's the fattest boy in the school."

"I won't be like him," Timmy said. He was angry.

"Yes, you will."

"No, I won't."

"Don't shout," Mrs Blake said. "Timmy's hungry, so he can eat some more. He hasn't had enough yet. There's no bread in the house, so you can have some biscuits, Timmy," his mother said. And she went out of the room and *fetched* some biscuits. She brought a plate full of biscuits. "You can have one or two biscuits," his mother said and she went out of the room. Then she came back. What did she see? The plate was empty! "My goodness!" she cried. "Timmy has eaten all the biscuits! Timmy, you'll burst. You'll be sick!"

"I don't want any more food, mum," Timmy said. "I don't feel very well."

"He doesn't look very well, either," Wendy said. "Look at him. He looks ill."

"What's the matter Timmy?" Mrs Blake said. "Do you feel sick?"

"No, mum. Something terrible's happened."

"What?" Mrs Blake asked. "What's happened, Timmy?"

"He's going to be sick and it serves him right, the greedy boy," Wendy said.

"Quiet, Wendy," Mrs Blake said.

"I'm not going to be sick," Timmy said.

"What's the matter with you then?"

"Nothing," Wendy said. "Nothing's the matter with him."

"Quiet, Wendy," Mrs Blake said.

Everything was quiet. Then Timmy got up. He had his hand on his *tummy*. "Mum," he said softly. "I've eaten too much and I've burst. I've really burst."

Mother looked at Timmy and laughed. Then Timmy's *pants* fell down and everybody laughed.

"He really has burst," Wendy said. "Look, his pants have fallen down."

"Don't be silly," Mrs Blake said. "You can't really burst."

"What's happened to me then?" Timmy asked.

Mrs Blake looked at Timmy's pants. "You've eaten too much, Timmy," she said, "and the *elastic* on your pants has broken!"

New Roller-skates

Sandy and Sue sat in the living-room and watched television. They watched it for a long time. "What are you doing, children?" mother asked. "Haven't you got anything to do?"

"No, mum," Sue said. "We've done our homework and now we've got nothing to do."

"Play with something," mother said.

"We've got nothing to play with," Sandy said.

"Nothing to play with!" mother cried. "There are so many toys in your rooms! What about your new roller-skates?"

"We can't skate," Sandy said.

"Well," mother answered, "you must learn to skate. You can't sit here and watch television all evening."

"Come on, Sandy," Sue said. "Let's go out into the street. We can try to skate."

Sandy and Sue are learning to skate. They can't skate very well and they always fall down. They'd both like to skate very much. Sandy put on his roller-skates and walked carefully.

"I'd love to skate, Sue," he said.

"I'd love to skate, too," Sue said. She put on her roller-skates and walked very carefully. "I'm ready," Sue said. "I'll try to skate to you and you can try to skate to me."

"All right," Sandy said.

"Whoops!" Sue cried. "I can't stand up."

"Whoops!" Sandy cried. "Neither can I!"

Suddenly, there was a loud *crash!* Sandy and Sue fell down.

"Did you hurt yourself, Sandy?" Sue asked.

"No," Sandy said.

"Neither did I," Sue answered.

They both sat on the ground and laughed. Suddenly, Sue looked up. "Oh, look!" she cried. "Here comes Alan Blake."

Alan Blake has a new bike. He can ride it very well, but he likes to show off. "Look at me," Alan said. "Look, *no hands!*" Alan waved both his hands at them. He rode very well and he didn't fall.

"That's dangerous," Sandy said.

"No, it isn't. It's easy," Alan Blake said. Then he looked at Sandy and Sue. "What are you two doing?" he asked. "Why are you sitting on the ground?"

"We're learning to skate," Sue said. "We fell down."

"Ha! Ha!" Alan laughed. "Can't you skate? I can skate. It's easy to skate. Anyone can skate. Lend me your skates, Sue." Alan got off his bike and Sue gave him her skates. Alan put them on and Sue watched him. Now, of course, Alan can't skate. He has never skated in his life. He is showing off. Sue knows this and she's smiling. Alan stood up carefully. "It's easy to skate," he said. "Remember to go like this."

"That's just what we want to do," Sandy said. Suddenly, there was a loud crash and Alan fell down.

"Whoops!" he cried. "I'm falling."

Sandy and Sue laughed. "Don't show off," they said.

"It's easy to skate, isn't it?" Sue said.

"I'm sorry," Alan smiled. "I can't skate, really, but I can ride a bike. I really can ride very well."

"I've got a good idea," Sandy said. "You can ride your bike, and we can wear our skates and you can pull us."

The children *tied* the end of Sue's skipping-rope to Alan's bike. Alan got on his bike and rode. Sue held the other end of the rope. Then it was Sandy's turn.

"It's good fun," Sandy cried. "We'll learn to skate soon."

At the Park Last week, Sandy, Sue and Alan went to the

85

park. It's very nice at the park and the children like to play games there. There was an old *keeper* at the park for many years. He was a very kind old man. He loved children and he often played games, too. But the kind old keeper died last year. There's a young man there now. He's a nasty fellow.

"Where's the old keeper?" Sue asked.

"Didn't you know?" Sandy said. "He died last year. There's a new keeper here now."

"I'm very sorry to hear that," Sue said.

"I'm sure that we can still play games on the grass," Sandy said. "We always play games on the grass."

The children ran on to the grass. "Throw the ball to me," Sandy cried. "Remember to throw it high up."

Just then, they heard a loud cry. "Hey! What are you doing?" It was the new keeper. He was very angry. "What are you children doing?" he called. "Look at this sign. It says, KEEP OFF THE GRASS. Can't you read?"

"But we always play on the grass," Sandy said.

"I don't care," the new keeper said. "You're not allowed to play on the grass any more."

Sandy, Sue and Alan went off the grass. They were sorry to stop their game. The new keeper smiled.

"Look," Sue whispered. "He's pleased that we must get off the grass."

Now there's a big lake in the middle of the park, so the children went to it. "I've remembered to bring some bread with me," Sue said, "so we can feed the ducks." The children began to feed the ducks. But suddenly the new keeper appeared. They were all surprised to see him.

"Look at that sign," he shouted. "DO NOT FEED THE DUCKS. You're not allowed to feed the ducks. Can't you read?"

"But we always feed the ducks," Sue said.

"I don't care," the keeper said. "You're not allowed to feed the ducks any more."

Poor Sandy! Poor Sue! Poor Alan!

"What can we do now?" Sue said. "Let's sit on that seat." The children went to the seat. "Oh dear!" Sue said. "I don't think that we can sit here. Look at that sign. It says, WET PAINT."

"No," Alan said. "I don't want green stripes on my trousers."

"Neither do I," Sandy said.

"And I don't want green stripes on my skirt, either," Sue said.

"Well, what can we do?" Alan asked.

"I know!" Sandy cried. "We can stand beside the lake and watch the ducks."

The children went to the lake. On the way there, they saw the keeper. The keeper spoke to a lady in a car.

"You can't park here," he said. "It says, NO PARKING, so you mustn't park here. You're not allowed to."

The poor lady was sorry to leave. "There are always cars here," Sandy said. "The old keeper let anyone park here." The children stood beside the lake. Then they saw some people in a boat. The new keeper saw the people, too.

"You can't sail on the lake," the new keeper cried. "It says, NO BOATS. Can't you read?"

"But we always sail on the lake," the people answered.

"I don't care," the new keeper said. "You're not allowed to." The new keeper was very cross. He shouted and waved his arms. Then, suddenly, he fell into the lake. The people in the boat laughed. "It serves you right," they said. And Sandy, Sue, and Alan laughed, too. "You can't swim here," a man in the boat said. "Look at that sign. It says, NO SWIMMING. Can't you read?"

The Pot of Stew

Last Saturday mother didn't feel very well, so father called the doctor.

"Well, Mrs Clark," the doctor said. "You've got a temperature and you mustn't get up. You must stay in bed for three days."

"Three days!" mother cried. "I can't stay in bed during the week-end. Who'll *look after* the family?"

"I'm afraid they'll have to look after *themselves,*" the doctor said. He gave mother some medicine and left the house.

Then father came into the room. "Well, dear?" he asked. "How are you?"

"The doctor says I've got a temperature," mother said. "He thinks I've caught a bad cold and he says I must stay in bed."

"Of course," father said.

"But I can't stay in bed," mother said. "Who'll look after you all? I must get up. I'll have to *do the shopping.*"

"You certainly won't get up!" father cried. "You're not allowed to get up. You must stay in bed. Sue, Sandy and I shall look after you."

Father went downstairs and spoke to Sue. Then they both went shopping. They bought lots of things. They bought meat, fruit and vegetables. "I hope you can cook," father said to Sue.

"I'm learning at school," Sue said. "I can't cook very well yet."

"Well," father laughed, "we've both got to cook this week-end."

They arrived home and father went up to see mother.

"Jim," mother said. "I'm going to get up. I must go to the shops to buy some fruit, some meat and some vegetables."

"You needn't worry," father said. "We've already bought the food for the week-end. Now Sue, Sandy and I shall *prepare* the lunch. Come on, Sandy. Come on, Sue," father called.

"Dad," Sandy said. "I'm afraid I can't help you in the kitchen."

"Why, Sandy?"

"Because I've got to write two hundred *lines.*"

"Two hundred lines!" father cried. "What do you have to write?"

"I have to write: 'I mustn't talk during the lesson'."

Sandy sat down. He wrote "I mustn't talk during the lesson" again and again and again and again.

Father and Sue went into the kitchen. "We can make a nice *stew*," father said. "Cut up some onions and some potatoes, Sue, and I'll prepare the meat."

Sue peeled the potatoes and cut them into small pieces. Then she peeled the onions. Suddenly father looked at her. "Why are you crying?" he asked.

"Guess!" Sue laughed. "It's these onions!"

Father laughed. "You mustn't cry, Sue," he said.

They put the meat, the potatoes, the onions and some carrots into a pot. It was a tremendous amount of food. Then they cooked the food for a long time. Father looked into the pot.

"What's it like?" he asked.

"I'll taste it," Sue said.

"Oh!" she cried. "It doesn't taste very nice."

"What's the matter with it?"

"We've forgotten to put any *salt* in it."

"Now where's the salt?" father said. He looked round the kitchen and found a big jar. Suddenly, Sue saw him.

"Oh, dad!" she cried. "You mustn't put that into the stew. That isn't salt! It's sugar! Here's the salt."

Then Sandy came into the kitchen. "I mustn't talk during the lesson. I mustn't talk during the lesson," he said. "Is dinner ready, yet, Sue?"

"Yes, and please don't talk now. We're busy,' Sue said.

Father and Sue prepared a *tray* of food for mother and took it to her room.

"Mm," she said. "It's *delicious*. You must give me the *recipe*."

"We didn't use a recipe," father said. "We just put some meat and vegetables in a pot and cooked them together."

"We're glad you like it, mum," Sue said.

"What are you going to cook for tonight and tomorrow?" mother asked.

"We don't have to cook anything at all," father said. "We've cooked enough food for a week! We're going to eat stew all today, tomorrow, and every day during the week!"

"Oh!" Sandy cried. "Please get well soon, mum!"

Just One of Those Days!

Last Monday was a holiday. Father didn't have to go to work and the children didn't have to go to school. Mother got up early, but father and the children got up very late.

"You're all very lazy today," mother said. "How are you going to spend the day today? Well, children?"

"We don't know," Sue answered.

"Why don't you do your homework, Sue?" mother asked.

"I should do my homework," Sue said, "but I don't feel like it. It's a holiday."

"What about you, Sandy?" mother asked. "Why don't you finish that book? You're reading it, aren't you?"

"Yes, mum. I should finish it, but I don't feel like it."

"You are lazy today," mother said.

Then father came into the room. "How are

you going to spend the day, Jim?" mother asked.

"I don't know," father said.

"Will you repair the fence please?"

"Oh," father complained. "I should repair it, but I don't feel like it."

"Isn't our breakfast ready yet?" Sandy asked.

"No, it isn't," mother answered.

"You ought to have got it ready," Sandy said.

"Sandy!" father said. "You shouldn't talk like that to your mother."

Mother got very cross. "It's a holiday for you," she said, "but it isn't a holiday for me. You don't have to go to school or to work but I have to cook breakfast, lunch and dinner. I have to iron the clothes, too."

"I'm sorry, mum," Sandy said.

"We're all *bad-tempered* this morning," father said. "We can all go out."

"That's a good idea," mother said.

"Hurrah!" the children shouted.

"But I want to have a bath first," father said.

"And I want to iron some clothes," mother said.

Mother stayed in the kitchen and ironed some clothes. The children played in the garden. Half an hour later father went out into the garden, too. "We're ready now," he called. "Let's all get into the car."

The family got into the car and father drove into the country.

An hour later, mother said, "Jim, I think I forgot to turn off the electricity. I ironed some clothes and I should have turned off the electricity, but I forgot."

"My goodness!" father cried. "We must go back at once. Father turned back. He was very bad-tempered. He complained all the way home. "You should have turned off the electricity!" he said. "Perhaps the house is burning."

Father drove very fast and soon the family

arrived home. They opened the front door quickly and mother rushed into the kitchen.

"Well?" father asked.

"It's all right," mother said. "I turned it off."

"I'm glad," father said.

Then Sandy went into the bathroom. "Mum!" he called. "The bathroom's full of water."

"Oh!" father cried. "I had a bath. I should have turned the tap off, but I forgot."

There was water everywhere. They all worked very hard and cleaned up the *mess*.

"It's been a very bad day," mother said. "We've all been bad-tempered and so many nasty things have happened today."

"Life's like that sometimes," father said. "Everything is fine and suddenly, everything is very bad and we all feel unhappy. It was just one of those days!"

Father and Sandy Go Fishing

Last Sunday, father and Sandy got up very early.

"Where are you going, Jim?" mother asked.

"Sandy and I are going fishing," father said.

Father woke Sandy up. Then he went into the kitchen and made some sandwiches. Sandy came into the kitchen, too. "What must we take with us, dad?" he asked.

"We've got to take our *fishing-lines,* a basket and some sandwiches," father said.

"We needn't take a basket," Sandy said and smiled. "We won't catch any fish."

"Yes, we will," father said.

Father and Sandy left home. Father had to drive to the seaside. They arrived at the seaside and both went on to the *pier*. "We can fish from the end of the pier," father said. They both put some *bait* on their *hooks*. Then they threw their lines into the sea.

"The fish are biting, dad," Sandy said. He pulled in his line quickly.

"Did you catch anything?" father asked.

"No," Sandy said. "I needn't have pulled my line in. I pulled it in for nothing."

"No, you didn't, Sandy," father laughed. "The fish have eaten your bait. You've got to put some more bait on your hook." Sandy had to pull the line in and had to put more bait on his hook. "You mustn't feed the fish, Sandy," father laughed. "You must catch them!"

"The fish are hungry and so am I," Sandy said. "May I have a sandwich please, dad?"

"Of course," father said. "I'll have one, too." Sandy and father ate two sandwiches each. Suddenly, father pulled his line. "There's a fish on the end of it," he cried. "I can feel it."

"Pull it in, dad," Sandy cried.

"I must be careful," father said. He pulled the line in carefully and Sandy looked into the water. He could see a *silver* fish on the end of the line. Then father pulled it up.

"Look at it, dad," Sandy laughed. "It's very small. It's a baby."

"You're right, Sandy," father said. "We mustn't keep this fish. It's too small." Father threw the fish back into the sea.

Suddenly, Sandy felt his line. It was very heavy. "There's a big fish on the end of my line!" Sandy shouted. He pulled it in quickly. Father looked into the water. He could see a big silver fish.

"Sandy!" he cried. "You've caught a big one! Be very careful!"

Sandy was very *excited*. He pulled in the line suddenly.

"Oh!" father cried. "You shouldn't have pulled the line like that. You should have pulled it in slowly!"

Poor Sandy! He lost the fish. "It was very big," he said. "I'll tell mum, but she won't believe me. That fish was thirty centimetres long."

"You oughtn't to have pulled the line like that, Sandy,". father said. "But never mind."

The day passed, but father and Sandy didn't catch any more fish. "We must go home now," father said.

"What will mum say?" Sandy asked.

"She'll laugh," father said. "We're not very good fishermen."

At the end of the pier they saw a real fisherman. He had a big sign. It said "Nice *Fresh* Fish".

"We can buy some fish, Sandy," father said. He bought lots of nice fresh fish. Then they went home.

Mother looked into their basket. "My goodness!" she cried. "Did you catch all those fish?"

Father looked at Sandy and Sandy looked at father. They both laughed. "That's our secret, isn't it, Sandy?" father said. They both laughed again and mother didn't know why!

The Remarkable Rooster

Mr Blake's garden looks very nice now. He has been working very hard for a long time. He has been working in his garden since last September. Mr Blake has planted trees and flowers. He has planted vegetables, too. He has mended the old fence. Of course, he hasn't finished yet. He's been working in the garden for a long time and he's still working hard. In one corner of the garden Mr Blake has built a *hen-run*. He has five *hens* and they *lay* lots of eggs. Last week Mr Blake arrived home with a *rooster*. The rooster looks very fine indeed. Alan, Wendy and Timmy call him 'Doodle'. Do you know why? They call him 'Doodle' because he *crows* every morning. Every morning everyone in the neighbourhood hears Doodle. *"Cock-a-doodle-doo!* Cock-a-doodle-doo!" Doodle has been waking Sandy and Sue up every morning. But they don't mind.

Timmy likes Doodle very much. He goes into the hen-run every day. Last Sunday he ran into the house and called his father. "Dad!" he cried. "Come to the hen-run quickly!"

"What's the matter, Timmy?" Mr Blake asked.

"It's something very strange," Timmy said. "Doodle's *laid an egg*."

"Laid an egg!" Mr Blake cried.

"Don't be silly, Timmy. Roosters don't lay eggs!"

"But he has laid an egg. Come and see," Timmy said.

Mr Blake went to the hen-run. Doodle was sitting in the hen-run and Mr Blake picked him up. There was an egg under the rooster.

"See," Timmy said. "Doodle's sitting on an egg. He's laid it."

"This is very strange," Mr Blake said. He looked at the rooster again. "He can't be a hen. Surely he isn't a hen!"

The next day Timmy called his father again. "Dad!" Timmy said. "Doodle's laid another egg."

"Don't be silly!" Mr Blake said.

"Come and see," Timmy said.

Mr Blake went to the hen-run. He found an egg under the rooster again. "I can't understand it. Perhaps Doodle's really a hen. He may be a hen. I'm not sure."

The next day Doodle laid another egg. "This is very strange indeed," Mr Blake said. "This rooster's been laying eggs since Sunday."

Soon the neighbours heard about this *remarkable* rooster. "Is it true?" they asked. "It can't be true! It must be a mistake! Rooster's don't lay eggs."

Mr Spencer is a *vet*. He lives near the Blakes. He heard about the remarkable rooster, too, so he came to Mr Blake's house to see Doodle. "I've heard about Doodle," Mr Spencer said. "May I see him please?" Mr Spencer had a look at Doodle and laughed. "He's a rooster, Mr Blake," he said, "and he isn't laying eggs."

"But he is," Mr Blake said. "He's been laying eggs every day this week."

"No," Mr Spencer said. "Someone's playing a trick on you. Who collects the eggs from the hen-run every morning?"

"Timmy," Mr Blake said. Then he called Timmy.

"Timmy," Mr Spencer said, "tell me about these eggs."

Timmy laughed and laughed. "I played a trick on dad," he said. "I've been putting an egg under Doodle every day this week."

Mr Spencer laughed and so did Mr Blake. The neighbours heard the story and they laughed, too. "Perhaps he'll lay a *golden* egg one day," Timmy said.

The Ghost Story

"Your father and I are going out this evening, Sue," mother said. "We shan't come home late. We'll be home at 10 o'clock."

"That's all right, mum," Sue said. "Sandy and I will be all right alone. We'll do our homework and then we'll read and go to bed."

"It's Saturday night," father said. "So you can stay up a little later."

"All right, dad," Sue said.

Mother and father said goodbye to the children. Sandy and Sue did their homework. They finished it at 8.0 o'clock.

"What shall we do now, Sue?" Sandy asked.

"We can read," Sue said. "I'm going to read an *exciting ghost story.*"

"Please read it to me, Sue," Sandy said.

The children sat down in the living-room and Sue got her book of Ghost Stories. Sue began to read a story. The name of the story was 'The Ghost Returns'. Sandy listened quietly. It was very quiet in the living-room and it was very dark outside.

" 'Then,' Sue read, 'the clock *struck 12.0.* It was midnight. James Cooper was alone in the *haunted* house. He was waiting for the ghost. The ghost should have come at midnight. It's after midnight, Jim thought. I haven't see a ghost yet. I don't believe in ghosts. I think I'll go to bed. Just as Jim was going upstairs, he heard a sound. It was a knock at the door. Jim stopped and listened. Then he heard the sound again. Jim went downstairs and opened the door. There was no one there. It can't have been a ghost, Jim laughed. It must have been the wind. He shut the door and went upstairs. Then he heard the knock again. This is silly, Jim said. It must be a cat. He looked up and saw something at the top of the stairs. It was white. It didn't move. Then Jim heard the knock again . . .' "

"Oh, stop it, Sue," Sandy cried. "Please don't read any more."

"Don't be silly, Sandy," Sue said. "It's only a story."

Suddenly, the children heard a knock at the front door. It wasn't very loud. "Listen, Sue!" Sandy whispered.

"I didn't hear anything," Sue answered. "It must have been the wind."

Then there was another knock. It was louder this time.

"Did you hear it, Sue?" Sandy asked. "What shall we do?"

The children went to the door quietly and listened. "I'm not going to open the door," Sandy whispered. "It might be a ghost."

"It can't be, Sandy," Sue said. "Don't be silly."

Then there was another knock. It was louder!

"Who is it?" Sue called.

"Open the door please, Sue," a voice said. "It's me."

"It's mum and dad," Sue said and she unlocked the door.

"We forgot our key," father said. "We didn't knock loudly because we didn't want to disturb you. It's ten o'clock. I was sure you must both be in bed."

Sandy and Sue gave their parents an extra big *kiss*.

"What's the matter, children?" mother said. "You both look *frightened*."

"We were frightened, but we aren't now," Sue said. "We were reading an exciting ghost story."

"It was too exciting for me," Sandy said. "I don't want to hear another ghost story for a long time!"

The Pound Note

Yesterday morning there was a knock at the door. Sue opened the door. "Who was it, Sue?" mother called.

"The postman who delivers our letters," Sue answered. "There's a parcel for you, mum, and there are letters for Sandy and me."

The letters were from grandmother and grandfather. Guess what they sent to Sandy and Sue. One pound each!

"That's a lot of money," mother said. "What are you going to do with it, Sue?"

"I'm going to put it in my money-box," Sue said.

"Don't be silly," Sandy said. "You can't put paper money in a money-box."

"Oh yes, I can," Sue said. "I'm going to fold it and put it in the money-box. I don't want to spend it."

"What are you going to do with your money, Sandy?" mother asked.

"I'm going to spend it," Sandy said. "May I spend it, mum?"

"Yes, you may, Sandy," mother answered. "But put your money in a safe place now. Don't lose it."

"No, I shan't lose it, mum," Sandy said.

On the way to school Sandy passed a toy shop. "Look at that glider," he said to Sue.

"Which glider?" Sue asked.

"The one which is near that electric train. I'm going to buy it," Sandy said.

"How much is it?" Sue asked.

"I don't know," Sandy said. "There's no price on it."

"Go in and ask, Sandy," Sue said.

Sandy went in and asked the price. It was 85 pence. Then he went into the street. "It's 85 pence," he said to Sue.

"Who did you ask?" Sue said.

"The man who is in the shop," Sandy answered.

"Are you going to buy that glider?" Sue asked.

"Yes," Sandy said. "I haven't got my pound with me. It's at home."

"Where did you put your pound?" Sue asked.

"In the pocket of my grey trousers. I changed my trousers this morning."

"That's not a safe place," Sue said.

"Of course, it is," Sandy said. "My grey trousers are at home and there's a pound in one one of the pockets."

"Well, my pound is in my money-box," Sue said.

Sandy was very excited. He thought about the glider all day at school. In the afternoon he hurried home. Mother was very busy. She was washing clothes.

"Mum," Sandy said. "I'm going to buy a glider which I saw in a shop. Where are my grey trousers?"

"Which grey trousers?" mother asked.

"The grey trousers which I was wearing yesterday," Sandy said.

"They're very dirty," mother said. "I'm going to have them cleaned."

"Yes," Sandy said, "but where are they?"

"They're in your room, I think," mother said.

Sandy looked in his room, but he couldn't find them. He looked everywhere. He looked in his wardrobe. He looked under the chair and under the bed, but he couldn't find his grey trousers anywhere. "I can't find them," he complained.

"I'm sorry, Sandy," mother said. "I made a mistake. I'm washing the clothes. I put your grey trousers in the *washing-machine* a moment ago."

"In the washing-machine!" Sandy cried. He looked very sorry. "Did you take anything out of the pockets, mum?"

"No, Sandy. Was there anything in the pockets?"

"Yes, mum. The pound which grandma and grandpa sent me. It's in the pocket!"

"Oh, dear," mother said. "Your trousers are in the washing-machine now. You should have put your money in a safe place not in one of your pockets!"

Poor Sandy! He nearly cried. He was terribly sorry. He wasn't careful and he lost his pound note and now he couldn't buy his glider.

The Family Photograph Album

Last Saturday, mother, father and the children looked at the family photograph *album*. Sandy and Sue love to look at all the old photos in the album. They love to hear mother and father tell them about the photos and about the people in them.

"Look at this photograph of grandma," Sue said. She pointed at an old, yellow photograph. "She looks very nice, doesn't she, mum? But her clothes are rather strange."

"Women used to wear very long skirts in

those days," mother said.

"I like grandma's large hat," Sue said.

"Look," mother said. "There's a photograph of the house I lived in when I was a girl."

"You lived there for ten years, didn't you, mum?" Sue said.

"What's happened to it now?" Sandy asked.

"I don't know," mother said. "Perhaps it's still there. It was a very nice house with large rooms. There was a big garden at the back and I used to play there with my friends years ago."

Sandy *turned over* a few pages of the album and saw a big ship.

"I like this big ship," Sandy said.

"Daddy and I had a holiday in South America years ago," mother said. "That's the *ship* we travelled on. Grandmother took that photo. Look at it carefully. You can see your father and me. We are standing at the side of the ship. We are waving."

"I can see you," Sue said.

"You weren't born then," mother said. "Look! Here's the first photograph of Sue. She was a lovely baby, but she used to cry a lot."

"Lovely baby," Sandy laughed, "— she still is!"

"You be quiet, Sandy Clark," Sue said. "Look at your photograph. You used to be an ugly baby."

"Now, now, children," mother said. "You mustn't quarrel. Sandy used to smile a lot when he was a baby. Look! There he is in his *cot*. He's smiling. And this is a photograph of the two of you. You are both smiling. You are both saying 'cheese' at the camera."

Sue turned over a few pages of the album. Then she saw a photograph of some boys. They were wearing shirts and *shorts*.

"What's this photo, dad?" Sue asked.

"That's a school photo," father said. "That's the football *team* I played in. Can you find me?"

The children looked at the photo carefully. "Is that you dad?" Sandy asked.

"Of course not!" father laughed. "Don't you know your own father? That's me there!" He pointed at a little boy in shorts. "I was in the team. I used to play very well. I used to be centre-forward."

"But you can't play now," Sue said.

"Of course I can," father said.

"Let's have a game," Sandy said.

Sandy and father went into the garden and Sandy kicked the ball to father. "You can be centre-forward, dad," Sandy said. "And I'll be goal-keeper."

"Ready, Sandy?" father called and he ran towards the ball.

He kicked it very hard, but the ball didn't go towards Sandy. It went towards the kitchen window. There was a loud *crash* and the window broke. "My goodness!" mother called from the kitchen. "You used to play football, Jim, but you can't play any more!"

Dreams!

When Sandy was having tea yesterday, Alan knocked at the door. Mother answered it. "Can Sandy come out and play please, Mrs Clark?" Alan asked.

"He hasn't finished his tea yet," mother said. "When he finishes his tea, he can come out and play."

Sandy was in the dining-room. He heard Alan at the door. "I'm coming, Alan," he called. "When I drink my milk, I'll come outside."

"Bring your football, Sandy," Alan said.

Sandy drank his milk quickly and went into the garden. "What shall we play, Alan?" Sandy asked.

"Let's play football," Alan said.

"All right," Sandy said. "I'll be centre-forward

and you can be goal-keeper."

"All right," Alan said. "I'll stand between these two trees and I'll try and catch the ball when you kick it. These two trees will be the *goal posts*."

The boys played for a long time. Sandy kicked the ball to Alan again and again, but Alan caught it every time.

"Whew!" Sandy cried. "I'm tired."

"You didn't get a goal," Alan said. "If you're tired, we can have a little *rest*.

"All right," Sandy said.

The boys sat down on the grass. "You're a very good goal-keeper, Alan," Sandy said.

"I'm going to be a goal-keeper when I *grow up*," Alan said. "When I grow up, I'll be famous. I'll earn a lot of money and I'll be rich. What are you going to be when you grow up, Sandy?"

"I don't know," Sandy said.

"You won't be a *footballer*, because you can't play very well," Alan said.

Sandy got cross. "Don't show off, Alan," he said. "When I grow up I'll be more famous than you. I'll be an astronaut."

"Don't be silly," Alan said.

"You'll see," Sandy said. "And if I'm an astronaut, I'll fly to the planets! When I'm famous, my name will be in all the newspapers."

"But I'll be more famous than you," Alan said. "Thousands and thousands of people will come and see me. I'll be goal-keeper in the England *team*. And I'll be rich too. I'll buy a big house and a fast car."

"I'll be richer than you," Sandy said. "If I'm an astronaut, I'll have my own rocket. I'll live on the moon."

"Don't be silly!" Alan said. "When you're an astronaut, you won't have your own rocket. Rockets cost a lot of money."

"Well, I'll have a rocket," Sandy said. "You'll

see."

"If you have a rocket," Alan said. "I'll have ten aeroplanes."

"If you have ten aeroplanes," Sandy said. "I'll *own* the moon. The moon will be mine. If you want to visit me, or to play football on the moon, perhaps I'll let you come in my rocket."

"Then I'll own the earth," Alan said. "If you want to visit me, perhaps I'll let you. I don't know."

Sue was listening to this *conversation*. "What a silly conversation," she said. "Alan Blake will own the earth when he grows up and Sandy Clark will own the moon. Ha! Ha! You boys are silly."

"We were only talking," Sandy said.

"When I grow up," Sue said, "I'll be an actress. I'll be rich and famous. I shall have my own sweet shop, too, and I'll eat all the sweets in it."

"Sweets!" Alan said. "That's a good idea. Let's buy some sweets. Have you got any money?"

The children looked in their pockets, but they didn't have any money. "All these dreams," Sue said, "and we haven't got enough money for a few sweets!"

Thank You For Your Present

Sandy and Sue have started school again. They went back to school three days ago, but their next door neighbours haven't returned from their holidays yet. Mr and Mrs Blake and their three children are still on holiday. Alan is the oldest child. Then there's Wendy. She's younger than Alan. And then there's Timmy. He's the youngest in the family.

"Aren't they lucky!" Sandy said to Sue. "They're having an extra holiday. When will they come home?"

"They'll come home tomorrow evening," Sue said. "Why are you asking?"

"Well, it's Alan's birthday tomorrow," Sandy said. "We ought to buy him a present. We can give it to him when he returns."

"That's a good idea, Sandy," Sue said. "What shall we buy?"

"Let's buy him something grown-up. Not a toy," Sandy said.

"We can buy a *tie* for him. He'll like that."

"Have you got any pocket-money left, Sandy?" Sue asked.

"Yes, I haven't spent my pocket-money yet."

"Well you can lend me some. I've got none. I spent it all," Sue said.

"All right," Sandy said. "But don't forget to *pay it back!*"

Sandy and Sue went to a shop near their home. They looked at a lot of ties, but it wasn't easy for them to *choose* one.

"I like this one," Sandy said.

"It's awful," Sue said. "Alan won't like that."

"What about this one?" Sandy asked. "It's rather nice."

"Yes, and it isn't too expensive," Sue said.

Sandy paid for the tie and they took it home. They *wrapped* it in bright red paper. "We can give it to Alan tomorrow," Sandy said.

"No, I've got a better idea," Sue said. "We can give Alan a *surprise*. We can leave it on the *doorstep*. We needn't put our names on it or anything. We can write 'With best wishes from us all'. Alan will know that the present is for him, but he'll have to guess that we gave it to him."

"All right, Sue," Sandy said. "But why must we write 'From us all'?"

"Well, the present is from you and me and mummy and daddy."

The children wrote 'With best wishes from us all' on the bright red paper. Then they took the present next door. Everything next door was quiet. There was no one at home, of course. The children went to the front door. There were two empty milk bottles in front of the door.

"Let's leave the present between those two bottles," Sandy said. "Then Alan will find it."

The next evening the Blakes came home and Alan came to see Sandy and Sue. "We had a lovely holiday," he said. "And we've already missed a few days of school." Alan talked and talked, but he said nothing about his present.

"It's your birthday today, isn't it, Alan," Sandy said.

"Yes," Alan answered.

"Happy birthday," Sandy and Sue said.

"Thank you," Alan said.

Sandy and Sue waited for Alan to say something about the present, but he didn't say anything. At last Sandy said, "Didn't you get our present."

"Present?" Alan said in surprise. "Which present?"

"Well, the present we left on your doorstep. We put it between two empty milk bottles."

"No." Alan said. "There weren't any empty milk bottles on the doorstep. The milkman left some milk for us this morning."

Suddenly, Alan remembered something and laughed. "Just a minute," he said. "There was a strange note from the milkman. The note said 'Thank you for your present'. We couldn't understand it, because we didn't leave a present for the milkman."

"That was our present!" Sandy and Sue cried.

Dear Aunt Ada

Sandy hasn't been doing very well at school this year. He hasn't been doing his homework and mother isn't very pleased with him. Now he isn't allowed to watch television when he comes home and he isn't allowed to play.

"You mustn't go near the television," mother said yesterday. "You have to stay in your room and do your homework."

"Do I really have to, mum?" Sandy asked.

"I'm afraid you do," mother said. "Now please go upstairs."

Sandy went upstairs slowly and went into his room. He sat at his desk. Then he picked up his heavy schoolbag. It was on the floor and it was full of books. Sandy looked at all the books sadly. "Maths," he said to himself. "I should do some of these problems, but I don't feel like it." Then he picked up another book. "History," he said. "I ought to read this book, but I don't feel like it". Then he picked up another book. "English," he said. "I should write a composition, but I'm not going to . . ." Sandy looked out of the window. He didn't do any work.

Suddenly someone knocked at the door. Sandy jumped up. "Who is it?" he called.

"It's me," a voice said. It was Sue.

"Just a minute," Sandy said. "I'm busy. I'm doing my homework."

Sandy looked in his schoolbag and pulled out the history book. He opened it up quickly and put it on his desk. Then he sat down and he looked very busy. "What are you doing?" Sue asked.

"I'm very busy," Sandy said. "I'm reading."

"What are you reading, Sandy?"

"History," Sandy said. "It's my favourite subject."

"Don't *tell lies*," Sue said and laughed.

"I'm not telling lies," Sandy cried crossly.

"You are," Sue said. "Look. Your history book is upside down. You aren't reading at all. You're terribly lazy, these days, Sandy," Sue said.

"I know," Sandy answered. "I should do my homework, but I don't want to."

Sue left the room. Then Sandy had an idea.

"I know," he said to himself. "I'll write a letter to *Aunt Ada*."

Sandy found a piece of paper and began to write his letter. Then his mother came into the room. "My goodness, you look busy, Sandy," she said. "What are you doing?"

"I'm writing a letter to Aunt Ada," Sandy said.

"But what about your homework," mother asked.

"I haven't done that yet. There's plenty of time."

"Do you want me to read you the letter, mum? Sandy asked.

"All right," mother said.

" 'Dear Aunt Ada,' " Sandy began, " 'I know I haven't written to you for a long time. I hope you are well. We are all very well. We have started school again and that's not much fun, but I don't mind because it will be my birthday soon. Thank you very much for your lovely present. I hope you will be able to come to my party this year. Love, Sandy.' "

"Lovely present?" mother asked. "Which lovely present?"

"Aunt Ada sent me a lovely present for my birthday last year," Sandy said.

"Sandy!" mother said. "Didn't you thank Aunt Ada for her present?"

"No," Sandy said. "I should have thanked her, but I forgot."

"And you are thanking her now," mother said.

"Yes," Sandy said. "It's my birthday next week and I don't want Aunt Ada to forget it. That's why I'm writing her a letter."

The QE 2

"Hurry up, children," father said. "We're leaving in a few minutes."

Sandy and Sue were still having their breakfast.

It was Saturday and they didn't have to go to school. They had both got up rather late.

"What's the hurry, dad?" Sandy said. "There's no school today."

"Don't you remember, Sandy?" father said. "We're going on an excursion today. We're going to Southampton."

"Of course!" Sue cried. "We had forgotten about that."

The children finished their breakfast quickly and ran out to the car. Mother sat in the front, next to father. Sandy and Sue sat in the back with Gretel, an au-pair girl from Austria. She had come to England to live with the Clark family. Father started the engine and drove away. While they were driving out of London, Gretel asked a lot of questions. She hadn't been out of London before and she was very excited.

"Where are we going?" she asked.

"We're going to Southampton," Sandy said.

"Where's that?" Gretel asked.

"It's on the south coast of England. It's a very big *port*," father said. "We're going to see the *QE 2* today."

"The QE 2?" Gretel asked. "What's that."

"That's the ship I told you about. It's the biggest *liner* in Britain."

"I know about the Queen Elizabeth and the Queen Mary," Gretel said, "but I don't know about the QE 2."

"The Queen Elizabeth and the Queen Mary are very old now. They don't sail to America any more," Sue said. "The new liner, QE 2, goes to America now."

"Are we allowed on the QE 2, dad?" Sandy asked.

"Yes, Sandy," father said. "Visitors are allowed on today. But we must all *keep together*. It's a very big ship and we mustn't get lost."

Gretel kept looking out of the window. "The

countryside is so green and beautiful," she said. "I haven't seen it before."

"It's green because it rains so much," Sue said.

The time passed very quickly and they soon arrived at Southampton.

It wasn't difficult to find the QE 2. She's a very big ship.

"Doesn't she look beautiful!" father said.

"I like that black funnel," Sue said.

There were a lot of people looking at the ship. Some of them were standing on the *quay*. Others were going up the *gangway*. Father went towards the gangway and the family and Gretel followed him. "Don't forget we must keep together," father said again.

The Clarks and Gretel went all over the ship. They saw the *ballrooms*, the dining-rooms and went into the ship's *lounges*. Then they saw some of the *cabins*. After that they went on to the *decks*. Father took a lot of photographs. The children liked the swimming-pools best. Time passed very quickly. Suddenly, they heard a bell.

"What's that, dad?" Sue asked.

Father looked at his watch. "My goodness," he said. "It's already a quarter to five. It's time for us to leave. Visitors aren't allowed on the ship after five o'clock. We must get off now." Father looked round. "Where's Sandy," he asked.

"He was here a moment ago," Sue said.

"He went down there," Gretel said.

Father went down some *steps* and they all followed him. Then an *officer* spoke to father. "I'm sorry, sir," the officer said. "Visitors must leave the ship now. It's nearly five o'clock. Would you go to the gangway please?"

"But I can't find my boy," father said. "He was here a minute ago."

The ship's officer smiled. "Don't worry, sir," he said. "We'll find him. Wait here please."

They all waited and waited, but Sandy didn't

arrive. The bell rang again. It was five o'clock. The visitors were all going down the gangway, but the Clarks and Gretel were still *on board*. Suddenly, a sailor appeared. He spoke to the officer. "Excuse me, sir," he said. "I found this young *chap* in the engine room."

"The engine room?" father cried. "Sandy, I told you . . ."

"I'm sorry, dad," Sandy said. "I got lost. I looked everywhere, but I couldn't find you."

"You're lucky we found you young man," the officer said. "We're sailing to America at 12.03 tomorrow."

"America!" Sandy cried. "I don't think I'm lucky. I'd like to go to America."

"You will one day," the officer smiled.

"Come on, Sandy," father said. "Back to London."

"He's a little *stowaway*," Sue said.

The Miss World Contest

Yesterday afternoon mother was in the garden. She was standing near the garden fence and talking to her next-door neighbour, Mrs Blake.

"What'll you be doing this evening, Marion?" mother asked.

"We'll be staying at home, Betty," Mrs Blake answered. "My husband wants to see the *Miss World Contest* on television. He watches it every year."

"That's funny," mother said. "We're staying at home this evening, too. Jim wants to see the Miss World Competition, too. He watches it every year, too. I can't understand why he likes to watch it."

"I can't understand why my husband likes to watch it either," Mrs Blake said. "It's a silly programme."

"You're quite right," mother said. "There are plenty of other nice programmes. Still, we'll both be watching the same programme, so why don't you come to our place. Come after dinner and have coffee with us. Then all of us can watch the same programme."

"That's very kind of you," Mrs Blake said. "We'll come at about eight-thirty. Will that be all right?"

"That'll be lovely," mother said.

"Goodbye for now," Mrs Blake answered.

"Goodbye, Marion," mother said.

Father came home at six o'clock as usual. He caught the five twenty-seven train from London. During dinner mother told him about the Blakes. "Marion and her husband are coming for coffee after dinner," mother said.

"Oh, are they?" father answered. He didn't look pleased. "I want to watch television tonight. I think there's an important programme on."

"You *mean* the Miss World Contest," mother said.

"Oh, is that what's on?" father asked.

"Don't *pretend* you don't know," mother said with a laugh. "And you needn't worry. The Blakes want to watch it, too. All of us will be watching it together."

The Blakes arrived at eight-thirty. Mother had the coffee ready and they all sat in the living-room and watched the programme. Father and Mr Blake didn't say anything during the programme, but both the women talked all the time.

"Which of those two girls do you prefer?" mother asked.

"I don't like either of them," Mrs Blake said.

"Look! There's another two, now," mother said. "Which of them do you like best?"

"Neither of them," Mrs Blake said. "The one on the left is so *skinny*. And look at the one on the right. Isn't she untidy? She hasn't even combed her hair. If she can win the Miss World Contest, then I can."

"So can I!" mother cried. "Many of these girls aren't pretty at all."

"You're quite right, Betty," Mrs Blake said. "They aren't ugly, of course, but some of them certainly aren't pretty. And all of them are so skinny! Did you read that piece in the paper today? One of these girls has been on a diet for five years because she wants to enter the Miss World Contest. Imagine!"

"I read about that," mother said.

"The winner gets a very big prize, too," Mrs Blake said. "She gets a lot of money and she travels round the world."

"Some of these girls get parts in films," mother said. "I can't understand why. None of them are actresses."

"Of course, they're not," Mrs Blake said. "All they can do is stand there and smile stupidly. Look at them now. They're all getting into one long line."

"Now let's have a good look at all of them," mother said. "Which one of them do you like best?"

Mrs Blake looked at the girls for a moment, then she said, "Well, Betty, I must say, I don't like any of them. They're all tall and skinny."

Then Mother turned to look at father and Mr Blake. Both of them were watching the programme. They were very quiet. "You men are both very quiet," she said. "Which of these girls do you prefer?"

"Don't ask them, Betty," Mrs Blake said. "They like all of them!"

An Accident

Both Sandy and Sue are very excited today. It's Sunday and they're expecting *visitors*. Mother's brother and his family are coming to see them. They all live in Scotland and they're going to drive to London. They're going to stay in London for a week. Today, they're going to have lunch with the Clarks. Mother's brother is a *jolly* man. His name is Douglas. He always tells jokes and stories. His wife's name is Karen. Douglas and Karen have two boys. Their names are Ron and Paul. They are twins and they're twelve years old. Sandy and Sue like their *uncle* and aunt very much. They like their *cousins* too. But Scotland is very far away and they don't often see each other. So today is a very special day. Everyone is very excited.

Mother is in the kitchen. She's getting the lunch ready. Uncle Douglas and his family like fish very much. Uncle Douglas often goes fishing in Scotland—he's a better fisherman then father! Mother has bought a large fish and she's going to serve it cold with *mayonnaise*. She's making the mayonnaise now. Sandy and Sue are in the kitchen. They're watching their mother.

"When Ron and Paul come," Sandy said, "We'll play football in the garden."

"No, you won't," mother said. "Directly they come, they'll have lunch. They'll be here at one o'clock. As soon as Uncle Douglas comes he'll want his lunch. He loves fish."

"It's a lovely fish, mum," Sue said.

"Yes," mother answered. "It's nearly ready now. I'll cover it with mayonnaise."

"Can we help you, mum?" Sandy asked.

"Why don't you both set the table?" mother said.

Sandy and Sue went into the dining-room and began to set the table. "We'll have a lot of fun when Uncle Douglas comes," Sandy said. "He'll tell us some funny stories. And Ron and Paul will play football in the garden. They can play very well."

Sandy pretended to kick a ball. He was holding a tray of glasses.

"Be careful, Sandy!" Sue shouted. "You'll

drop those glasses."

Suddenly there was a loud crash. Sandy dropped the tray and the glasses fell on the floor. "What's happening?" mother called. She hurried into the dining room. "Oh, Sandy!" she cried. "You've been very careless. There's broken glass everywhere. Now be careful please. Don't cut yourselves. We must pick up all this broken glass."

"I'm sorry, Mum," Sandy said. "It was an accident."

"Never mind," mother said.

They picked up all the broken glass, then mother returned to the kitchen. Suddenly the children heard a loud shout. "It's mum," Sandy said. "Quick, Sue. What's happened?" The children ran to the kitchen. Mother was almost *in tears*. She was holding a large dish with the fish on it. The fish was all in pieces. There were pieces of fish on the floor. "What's happened?" the children asked.

"The cat!" mother said. While mother was in the dining-room, Sue's cat, Ginger, had come into the kitchen and had begun to eat the fish!

"Oh, mum," Sue said. "Can't you do anything?"

"No, Sue," mother said. "Just look at it. I can't do anything. And it's Sunday. All the shops are shut. We can't buy another one. Look at the time. It's twenty past twelve. They'll be here in half an hour. What are we going to do?"

Now Sue was almost in tears. "It's your fault, Sandy," she said. "You and your silly football. You dropped the tray and mum had to leave the kitchen."

Then father came into the kitchen. Mother, Sue and Sandy looked very sad. They didn't have time to tell father about the fish because the telephone rang and he went out to answer it.

He returned a few moments later. "Douglas

won't be coming today. They had an accident on the way. It's nothing *serious*, but their car is in a garage. They'll be here tomorrow."

Mother, Sue and Sandy laughed. "We've had an accident, too," mother said, and she told father about the fish.

"That's a story Uncle Douglas will like very much," father said.

Blondin

Blondin was very famous in the 19th century.

Blondin wasn't his real name. His real name was Jean Francois Gravelet. He was French. He could walk on a tight-rope when he was five. When he was a small boy he often walked on his mother's clothes line. He was a wonderful acrobat. Blondin went to school in Lyons. When he left school, he joined a circus. Since he was a wonderful acrobat he quickly became the best performer in the circus. He was the star.

One day his circus went to the United States. Of course, Blondin and his family went too. They had a house near Niagara Falls and Blondin often used to go there on Sundays with his family. He liked to watch the water at the great falls. When he was there, he had an idea. He wanted to walk across the falls on a tight-rope.

A Mr Hamblin heard about Blondin's idea and he offered to pay for a rope. The rope cost $1300 which was a lot of money in those days. You can imagine how long it was! Workmen put up the long rope across the Niagara. They fixed it at each end with smaller ropes to make it strong. Then Blondin got ready to walk across. Of course, the newspapers wrote a lot about this. Hundreds of people came in boats to see this great acrobat.

It was easy for Blondin to cross on the rope. He held a long *balancing pole* and walked across without any trouble at all! He repeated this act many times and became very famous. Large crowds always gathered to watch him. Blondin decided to make the *act* more difficult. Sometimes he used to go across *blindfold*. Sometimes he used to go across on *stilts*. Once he pushed a wheelbarrow across. Another time he went across blindfold while he was pushing the wheelbarrow —with someone in it! Blondin used to lie down on the rope or do *somersaults* on it. Sometimes he used to cook an omelette on it!

It wasn't always easy. There were some bad moments before the famous crossing with Colcord, his manager. Once when he was going across, one of the small ropes which held the big rope broke. The big rope swung terribly. But Blondin *kept his balance*. The rope swung for one minute and Blondin waited till it stopped. Then he continued to cross. The crowd *clapped* and cheered. The *Prince of Wales* was watching Blondin through a telescope at the time. When Blondin arrived at the other side, the Prince sighed with relief. "Thank goodness that's over," he said. He then congratulated the great acrobat.

You know about the crossing with Colcord. This was the most dangerous crossing of all. Blondin had to stop six times during the crossing. But as he was a wonderful acrobat, he went across safely. Colcord was terrified, but Blondin kept his balance. He really was the greatest tight-rope walker who had ever lived. He was born in 1824 and he died in 1897.

Christmas Eve

It's *Christmas Eve*. The Clarks have been very busy today. Father came home from work at midday. He has been helping mother. There will be a lot of visitors in the house on Christmas Day. Grandmother and grandfather will be coming and so will uncle Douglas and his family. The Clarks will have a big Christmas party.

Mother has gone into the kitchen to get the turkey ready. Father has gone into the dining-room to set the table. Sue has gone into her room to *wrap* her presents. She has locked her door so that no one will see her. Sandy has gone into his room to wrap his presents. He has locked his door so that no one will see him. Gretel is in the kitchen with mother. She is helping her.

Christmas cards have been arriving all the week and Sue has been collecting them. She has joined them all together with ribbon. She has hung the cards across the living-room in order to decorate it. They look very pretty.

Gretel has received lots of cards and letters from her friends in Austria. This morning she received a parcel from her parents. She wanted to open it and was so excited she could hardly wait. She didn't open it, of course. She put it under the Christmas tree. There are lots of presents under the tree now.

At dinner time this evening, Sandy was so excited he could hardly eat. "I'm not hungry, mum," he said. "I don't want anything to eat. I'm going to sing carols with my friends this evening. We'll eat something then."

"You ought to eat something now," mother said, "so that you won't get hungry this evening."

"I'm going to sing carols, too," Sue said. Sandy and I and some of our friends are going to collect money for charity."

When they finished their dinner, Sandy and Sue put on their coats. It was very cold outside. "Put on your *scarves* and *gloves*, too," mother said, "so you won't catch colds. It's freezing outside."

Sandy and Sue left the house and mother, father and Gretel stayed at home. Mother, father and Gretel went into the living-room.

"Is everything ready?" father asked.

"No," mother said, "but I'm not going to do

any more work today. I'm going to sit down and have a rest."

"I must fill the children's stockings," father said.

"You can't do that until they go to bed," mother said. "They're singing carols and they won't go to bed until late."

Suddenly there was a knock at the door. Father opened it. There were some children at the door. They sang a carol and father put some money in a box. These children were collecting money for charity too. When they finished, father went back to the living-room.

The time passed very quickly. "It's ten o'clock," mother said. "Sandy and Sue haven't come back yet. They're very late."

Suddenly there was a knock at the door. "Please open the door, Jim," mother said. "They must be carol singers."

They were carol singers. Guess who! Sandy and Sue of course. This is the carol they sang:

Silent night, holy night,
All is calm, all is bright,
Round yon Virgin, mother and child.
Holy infant so tender and mild,
Sleep in heavenly peace.
Sleep in heavenly peace.

Father put some money in Sue's box. "This box is so heavy, I can hardly hold it!" Sue said.

"And I'm so tired, I can hardly stay awake," Sandy said. "A merry Christmas, a happy New Year and goodnight to you all!"

The Pot of Gold

This story is about a farmer who was in prison. Even though this farmer was in prison, he wasn't a bad man. He hadn't done anything wrong. At this time the King's men were collecting money. The King needed money so that he could fight his wars and the people had to pay a lot of taxes. Now this farmer didn't have any money. He told this to the

King's men. When they came to his house, he said, "I can't give you any money. I am such a poor man I've hardly got enough to live."

The King's men laughed. "You don't expect us to believe that," they said. "We've heard you're so rich that you've got a pot of gold." They looked in every room in the house, but even though they didn't find anything, they arrested the poor farmer and put him in prison. "You will stay there until we receive the pot of gold," they said.

The poor farmer was very sad. He hadn't done anything wrong. While he was in prison he thought about his farm. His wife couldn't dig the fields by herself. One day he received a letter from his wife. She wrote, "I am so worried about our farm. It's nearly spring. It's time to plant the potatoes. I must dig up the fields." The farmer read this letter sadly. What can I do? he thought. Then he smiled. He had had a good idea. He wrote a letter to his wife. "Don't dig the fields," he wrote. "That is where my pot of gold is. Don't plant the potatoes until I tell you to."

The farmer gave this letter to the prison *guard*. "Please send this letter to my wife," he said. Now, of course, the prison guards read all the letters which the prisoners wrote and received. They had read the letter from the farmer's wife and now they read the farmer's answer. "Mm," they said. "This sounds very interesting. It looks as though this farmer really is a rich man. He writes that there is a pot of gold in his fields."

"He doesn't say which field," another guard said. "This farmer has got lots of fields."

"It doesn't matter," the first guard answered. "We know there's gold in his fields. He has hidden it there."

Two weeks later, the farmer received another letter from his wife. "Something funny happened," his wife wrote. "Two weeks ago, about ten men came to our farm. They all had spades and they all began to dig our fields. They dug all our fields and now they've gone away. I can't understand it. It looks as though they were looking for something. What shall I do now?"

The farmer smiled when he read his wife's letter. He didn't feel sad now, even though he was in prison. He wrote a letter to his wife at once. It was very short. "These men have dug up our fields," he wrote, "so now you can plant the potatoes."

The Foolish Villagers (Part 1)

This is another traditional folk-story. It's a rather long story and has three parts. The story is about some *villagers* who lived several hundred years ago. These people did extremely *foolish* things. Were they really so foolish? Decide for yourself at the end of the story.

One day the head man of the village spoke to the village *elders*. "I've just received some bad news," he said. "I have heard that the King wants to come to our village with some *soldiers*. The King and his soldiers will stay in our village for several months. If they stay here, they will eat all our food. Next week, one of the King's officers will be coming to our village. The King will send him to find out about us. When the officer finds out about us, he will return to the King and tell him. Then the King and his soldiers will come here. This is very serious. What can we do?"

The head man and the elders talked about the visit of the King's officer for a long time. When they had decided what they should do, they called all the villagers together and told them. The villagers all returned to their homes and got ready for the visit of the King's officer.

A week later, the King's officer arrived at the village. He was riding a horse. He was tired, hungry and thirsty. I've been riding for nearly two days, he thought. I must have a rest, a meal and a drink. The first thing he saw in the village was a fine old *inn*. I'll go to that inn, he thought. It looks as if I can have a meal and something to drink there.

The officer went into the inn. "Good morning," he said. "May I have a meal and a glass of wine?"

"Of course, sir," said the *inn-keeper's* wife. "My daughter will get some wine for you. This is my daughter, Bessy. Bessy, go and get some wine for the gentleman." "Yes, mother," Bessy said. Bessy went down to the *cellar*. While she was away, her mother talked about her to the officer. "She's a fine girl," her mother said. "She's going to *get married* soon. I must tell you about the young man she's going to marry . . ." The inn-keeper's wife didn't finish her story. Suddenly they heard loud cries from the cellar. "Help! Help! Help! Mother! Father! Come quickly!" The inn-keeper's wife, her husband and the King's officer all rushed down to the cellar. The girl was crying and pointing at an *axe* that *was stuck* in a *wine-barrel* above her head. "I was filling a glass with wine, when I noticed that axe," the girl cried. "If it had fallen, it would have killed me."

The moment her mother noticed this, she began to cry, too. "Oh, my poor child," she said. "If the axe had fallen, it would have killed you. And if you were married, your poor husband would lose his dear wife." As soon as she heard this, the girl began to cry even louder.

Then the girl's father spoke. "Just think, my dear," he said to his wife, "If the axe had killed our dear daughter, her children would have lost their mother."

When the wife and daughter heard these words, they began to cry even louder. The inn-keeper began to cry too. "Imagine!" he said. "Those poor babies without their mother."

The King's officer watched them all the time and didn't say anything. At last he said, "Excuse me, but none of these things has happened. Why are you all crying? Perhaps I can help you." The officer pulled the axe out of the barrel.

At once the girl and her mother and father sighed with relief.

"Oh, thank you sir," the inn-keeper's wife said. "You have saved our daughter's life. You can stay at our inn as long as you like. You don't have to pay for your wine or your food."

"But I haven't done anything," the officer said.

"We shall never accept any money from you, sir," the inn-keeper said. "You have saved our daughter's life. Now come upstairs and have a meal. Bessy, bring a glass of wine for the gentleman."

Bessy hadn't turned off the tap in the wine-barrel and there was wine all over the floor. The officer looked at it and shook his head. Then he went upstairs with the inn-keeper and his wife.

The Foolish Villagers (Part 2)

Do you remember the story of the foolish villagers so far? The King's officer went to a village to find out about the people. He first stopped at an inn. The people there behaved very strangely. Well, the officer spent the night at the inn and the next day he went out to see the village and to meet some of the villagers.

As he was walking along the road he saw four men. They were sitting on the ground under a tree. "Good morning," the King's officer said. "You don't seem to be very busy this morning."

"We should be at work," one of the men said, "but we can't find our legs."

"Can't find your legs?" the King's officer cried. "What are you talking about?"

"Well, it's like this," one of the men said. "I climbed this tree to get a bird's nest. The nest was on a high branch. My friends were waiting for me under the tree. I told them I couldn't reach the nest. I told them it was too high up. 'Don't worry,' one of them said. 'I'll come up and help you,' so he climbed up on to the branch but he couldn't reach the nest, either. He told the other two men that the nest was too high up. He said he was going to climb down again. 'Don't do that,' the other two men said. 'We'll come up and help you.' So they climbed on to the branch too. We all stood on the branch and tried to reach the nest, but we couldn't. Then one of the men said we should jump up and down on the branch so as to shake down the nest. We all jumped up and down on the branch and it broke. We all fell on to the ground."

"Did you hurt yourselves?" the King's officer asked.

"No," the man said. "But look at our legs. They're *tangled up*. We can't find our own legs. My friend says these legs are his and those legs are mine, but I don't think they are. We've all been quarrelling about it."

"Dear me," the King's officer said. "That's very serious. Perhaps I can help you. If I helped you, you would be able to go to work."

"Can you really help us, sir?" the man said. "Please do."

The King's officer took a stick and began to beat the men's legs.

The men jumped up. They cried *in pain*. "You're hitting us," they said. "You shouldn't do that. We didn't hurt you."

The King's officer told them that he was sorry. He said it was the only way he could help them to find their legs. The men understood this and they thanked the officer very much.

The officer shook his head sadly and went on

his way. Suddenly he saw a man counting some men who were standing in a line. "What are you doing?" the King's officer asked.

"I'm counting these men," the *leader* said. The leader told the King's officer that twelve of them had gone into the woods to *hunt* and one of them had got lost. He said there were now only eleven men. He said he was very unhappy about this. He said that perhaps a wild animal had killed their poor friend.

"Really?" the King's officer said. "This is very serious. How many of you were there this morning?"

"Twelve," the leader said.

"And how many are there now?"

"Eleven," the leader said.

"I think I can find your lost friend," the King's officer said.

"Oh, thank you, sir," the leader said. "If you can find him, you will *do us a great favour.*"

"Well," the King's officer said. "You are the lost man. You have been counting your friends. That is eleven men. But you haven't been counting yourself."

"You're a very clever fellow," the leader said. "Thank you very much." Then he spoke to the men. "Men," he said. "Wild animals didn't kill our friend. He's *alive.*"

"Hooray!" the men shouted. "We're glad he's alive. Now we can go home."

The leader told the officer he was very happy now. He said they had looked everywhere for their friend and now they had found him. He was alive and well. The King's officer shook his head sadly and went back to the inn. At the inn he met the inn-keeper and his wife. "Come and have a meal," the inn-keeper said. "You don't have to pay for it because you saved our daughter's life."

"Where is your daughter, Bessy?" the officer

asked.

"She's in bed. She's crying," the inn-keeper said. "If the axe had fallen on her head it would have killed her."

The King's officer shook his head sadly and then he had his meal.

The Foolish Villagers (Part 3)

Do you remember the story of the foolish villagers? The King's officer went to a village to find out about the people, because the King wanted to bring his soldiers into the village. The people in this village behaved very strangely and the King's officer thought they were *mad*. This is the last part of the story.

The King's officer had just returned to the inn. He thought he would have something to eat. He asked the inn-keeper if he could have a meal. The inn-keeper prepared an excellent meal for the King's officer. He was glad to serve the officer. "You saved my daughter's life," the inn-keeper said. "I shall never forget that."

The King's officer shook his head sadly. He ate the meal and as it was still early in the evening, he decided he would go for a walk in the village. He left the inn and walked down the *main* street of the village. As he walked along he heard the great bell in the village church. It *struck* five times. "It's five o'clock," the King's officer thought. "I'll enjoy my walk, then I'll go back to the inn." About twenty minutes later, the officer met a man in the street. The man was counting *aloud:* "One thousand and seven, one thousand and eight . . ." the man counted. "What are you counting?" the officer asked.

"I'm counting the time," the man said. "The church clock struck one thousand and ten ago. Now the time is one thousand and eleven. One thousand and twelve, one thousand and thirteen

"What do you *mean*?" the officer asked.

"Every time the clock strikes I must count the time," the man said. "How will I know the right time if I don't count it? Now please don't *interrupt* me. 'One thousand and fourteen, one thousand and fifteen . . .'"

The King's officer didn't say anything. He thought it was very sad. Now he really knew that all the villagers were mad. He walked on slowly. He walked for a long time. It grew dark. It was a clear night. The moon was shining brightly. The village looked very beautiful.

Suddenly, the King's officer heard voices. He walked in the direction of the sound until he came to a small lake outside the village. There were about twenty villagers round the lake. They were all holding sticks. They didn't see the King's officer. They were shouting at each other. "Have you got it yet?" "Oh, I nearly got it that time!"

"Try again!" And things like that. The officer noticed they were all striking the water with their sticks. He thought they were trying to catch fish. He stopped and watched them. Several of them were crying. "What shall we do? Oh, what shall we do? We've lost it and we'll never be able to get it back again! Oh, what shall we do?"

The King's officer went up to them and asked, "What have you lost?"

"Oh, sir," they said. "A terrible thing has happened. The moon has fallen into the lake. We have been trying to get it out with our sticks, but we can't. The moon is right at the bottom of the lake. Don't you understand, sir? We've lost the moon. We've lost it. It's gone *forever*."

The villagers cried bitterly. The King's officer told them that perhaps he could find the moon for them. At first the villagers didn't believe he could, but the officer told them he certainly could. "Please, sir," they said. "Find it for us. We'll give you anything you want if you do."

The King's officer took one of the villagers by the arm and pointed up at the sky. "Look, there it is," he said. The villagers all looked up at the sky. Then they looked into the lake. The water was so muddy they couldn't see anything in the lake now. Then they all cheered. At last one of them spoke. "My friends," he said, "this kind man has put the moon back in the sky for us. How can we thank him?"

"I don't want anything," the King's officer said quietly.

The villagers asked the officer to accept something but he wouldn't. They all went home. They were laughing and singing, but the officer sadly returned to the inn. "Good night, sir," the innkeeper said to him. "You saved my daughter's life . . ." The officer didn't wait to hear the rest of the story. He went to bed.

The next day, he returned to the King and told him about these people. The King heard about these mad people and decided he wouldn't take his soldiers into the village after all. Were the villagers really mad, do you think?

The Rich Young Man

There was once a rich young man who lived in Greece. He was very *successful* in everything he did. He hadn't always been rich.. His mother and father had been very poor. He had had few toys to play with and very often he had hardly enough food to eat. When he was ten years old, his father died and his mother worked very hard to provide her son with food and clothing. A few years later his mother died too. He was only sixteen then. Before she died, his mother said, "I have nothing to leave you, my son. I haven't any money, I haven't any land and this house we are living in belongs to someone else. Your father and I were not lucky in our lives. We both worked very hard, but we didn't *succeed*. But you will succeed. You will be rich and successful. You will always be lucky."

The young man often remembered his mother's words. He often wondered if she could see him now. He often wondered whether she knew he had become so successful. At the age of sixteen he had left school. Now he was only twenty-five and he was already a *millionaire*. Though the young man lived in great *luxury*, he was often sad. His friends couldn't understand why. His closest friend asked him if anything was wrong.

"Not really," the young man answered. "I sometimes think I am too lucky, It's not right to be so lucky. I am afraid that one day I will lose everything. I want to do something which isn't lucky. I want to lose money *for a change*."

"I quite understand how you feel," his friend said. "You want to *prevent* bad luck. Now I have a *suggestion*. Here, in Greece, we don't grow *dates*. Why don't you buy a lot of dates and then take them to *Egypt* to sell them? If you did that you would lose money because dates are very cheap in Egypt."

The young man liked this idea very much. He knew that if he did this he couldn't fail to lose some money. He bought a lot of dates in Greece and took them over the sea to Egypt. When he arrived in Egypt he hired a lot of *camels* to take the dates to *Cairo*. He wanted to take them to Cairo to sell them in the market.

Meanwhile, the King of Egypt was on his way to Cairo with his *servants*. During the journey, the King lost a precious gold ring and told his servants that they had to look for it. "We must find it," he said. "It's very valuable—not because it costs a lot of money, but because it was the first present my wife ever gave me. She will never *forgive* me if I lose it. I wonder whether we will ever find it." The servants looked everywhere, but they couldn't find anything.

Suddenly, the King saw the young man in the distance and called to him. He wanted the young man to help him. The King saw that the young man was a foreigner. "Where have you come from?" he asked.

"From Greece," the young man answered. "I've come to sell these dates which I bought in Greece."

The King laughed. "Dates from Greece?" he said. "How much did they cost you?"

"One gold piece for each bag," the young man said.

"One gold piece for each bag!" the King cried. "You won't get a quarter of a silver piece for each bag in the market."

The young man had to explain. He knew he wouldn't get much money for the dates, he explained. That was why he had come to Egypt. "I've come here to lose money," he said. "I want to prevent bad luck. I won't be happy until I've sold these dates and lost some money. I'm afraid that even now I won't manage to lose any money."

The young man sat on the ground. "Everything I touch," he said, "turns to gold." As he said this he picked up a handful of earth and then felt something in it. "What's this?" the young man asked. "Look, I've found a gold ring."

The King smiled when he saw the lost ring. "Thank you," he cried. "You've found my ring. My servants have been looking for it for hours. I must give you a *reward*. How much did you say you paid for those dates? One gold piece for each bag? Then I will give you five gold pieces."

The young man tried to refuse the King's offer, but the King wouldn't listen. As he accepted the King's money, he remembered his mother's words again: "You will always be lucky." And he remained lucky till the end of his life.

The Wonders of Science

This story is about Sue. Sue sometimes *goes baby-sitting* and earns a little pocket-money. Her mother lets her do this. Some of the neighbours ask Sue to baby-sit for an hour or two during week-days. If it's Friday or Saturday, Sue may baby-sit a little longer. She enjoys it very much. She takes her homework to the neighbours' houses and works quietly. She never has any trouble with the children. "All the children in our neighbourhood are well-behaved," Sue says. "They go to sleep very quickly and they never give me any trouble. Sometimes they ask if they can have a glass of water, or they ask when their parents will come home, but they are never naughty."

Mrs Clark's neighbours like Sue to come to their homes. They *trust* her. They know she is very good with children. All the neighbours know Sue very well, but recently, some new neighbours moved in. They live at the bottom of the street. They're a young couple and they have a little three-year-old boy called David. They heard that Sue sometimes did some baby-sitting and they asked her whether she would come to their house for two hours last Friday night. They said they wouldn't be away long. They were going to visit some friends who had invited them home for coffee.

So last Friday Sue went to the new neighbours' house. They were a very pleasant couple. Sue liked them both very much. "My name's Kim Williams and this is my wife, Jane," Mr Williams said. "We're very glad you could come, Sue."

Then Mrs Williams told Sue about David. "Don't worry about him," she said. "He's very well-behaved. Sometimes he talks to himself before he goes to sleep, but he never causes any trouble."

Sue asked where David's bedroom was and Mrs Williams took her upstairs. Sue didn't go into the bedroom, but she could hear David.

David was talking to himself quietly.

Then Sue went downstairs into the living-room. "Oh, I must tell you, Sue," Mrs Williams said. "We have an *intercom system.*"

"A what?" Sue asked. She had never heard of this before.

"An intercom system. Look. There's a small *loudspeaker* here. If David cries you can hear him and you can speak to him. You don't have to go upstairs at all. We had it put in this morning."

"That's clever," Sue said. "Very useful."

"The *wonders of science,*" Mr Williams said.

"I'm afraid we must be going now, Sue. I hope you'll be all right."

"Oh, yes," Sue replied. "Enjoy yourselves."

"If you need us you can ring this number," Mrs Williams said. "Goodbye."

Sue sat down in a comfortable armchair. At first Sue thought she would watch television. Then she noticed the intercom loudspeaker. I must listen to David for a moment, she thought. Perhaps he's still awake. She turned on the loudspeaker. She could hear David. He was still talking to himself very quietly.

Sue listened for some time. She didn't want to disturb David, but she wanted to talk to him very much. I must tell him that I'm here, she thought. No, perhaps I oughtn't to. I wonder what I should do.

Perhaps Sue just wanted to play with the intercom system. We shall never know. Anyway she decided to speak to David very quietly. She wanted to tell him she was there. So she whispered into the loudspeaker, "David . . . David . . ."

Then she heard a very soft voice which answered, "What do you want, wall?"

The Soup of the Soup

This is another traditional story. *Once upon a time* there was a poor village high up in the mountains. Though the village was poor, the inhabitants were happy. They didn't have any *luxuries*, but they usually had enough to eat and enough to drink. The husbands usually managed to grow a few vegetables. They kept a few animals. They grew fruit and made their own wine. The wives helped their husbands in spring, summer and autumn and in winter they stayed indoors and wove material to make clothes for the family. Of course, all the villagers knew each other. They were all good friends and they rarely quarrelled among themselves. They were always glad to help each other. If anyone asked for help, no one asked why. They just went along and helped him.

Now one winter the weather was very bad indeed. Snow began to fall early in October—much earlier than usual. It continued to fall during the winter months. And it snowed in spring too. It was still snowing even in April. Everything was frozen. It was a problem even to get water. The villagers managed quite well up to about March. They had a little salted meat. They had fresh meat too. *Now and again* they had to kill an animal in order to eat. But now it was April and spring still hadn't come. There were no more animals to kill. Things were really very bad.

As I said, the villagers were good people. They rarely quarrelled. But there was one family which was especially kind. They were also very lucky because a visitor from another part of the country came to see them during April and brought them two fine *geese*. They were very large birds and Mara (that was the name of the lady of the house) wondered what to do with them. She asked her husband.

"What do you think we should do with these geese, Tor?" she asked.

133

"I think we should make some soup," Tor said. "Then we can invite all our friends to have some. Everyone can have something to eat, too."

And that's what Mara did. She made an enormous pot of soup and invited all her friends to come and have some. It was quite a party, as you can imagine. Of course, all the villagers didn't come, but quite a lot of them did. The geese were so enormous that everyone had some soup and then they all had something to eat. Mara had made a *delicious* soup and everyone enjoyed it very much. "It was so kind of you to ask us to come," they said.

When all the visitors had gone, Tor looked in the pot and said, "You see, my dear, all our friends had something to eat and there is still some soup left. There's no meat, of course, but there's some soup. We can drink this delicious soup for a few days. Oh," he sighed, "I wonder when the winter will go away."

The next day, just as Mara and Tor and their children were sitting down to dinner, there was a knock at the door. It was a stranger and Tor asked him to come in. Mara and Tor didn't know this man, but, of course, they invited him into their house. "I'm a friend of *so and so*," the stranger said, naming a villager whom Mara and Tor knew well. "I heard you have made some lovely *goose* soup. May I have some please?"

"Of course," Mara said. "Come in. We're just having dinner ourselves. You're welcome to join us." And she gave the stranger a large plate of soup.

"That was delicious," the stranger said and he thanked them and left.

The next day, just as Mara and Tor and their children were sitting down to dinner, there was a knock at the door. It was a stranger and Tor asked him to come in. Mara and Tor didn't know this man, but of course, they invited him into their house. "I'm a friend of the friend of so and so," the stranger said. "I hear you have made some lovely goose soup. May I have some please?"

"You're welcome," Mara said and she gave the stranger a large plateful.

"That was quite good," the stranger said and he thanked them and left.

The next day, the same thing happened. A stranger knocked at the door just as they were going to have dinner. He wanted to try the goose soup too.

"I'm a friend of the friend of the friend of so and so," the man explained. Tor asked him to come in and Mara gave him a large plateful of soup.

The man tasted it and pulled a face. "I heard your soup was delicious, but this is just hot water," he complained. "It's the soup of the soup of the soup," Mara answered.

Stone Soup

Do you remember the story called 'The Soup of the Soup'? Here is another story about soup. It's called 'Stone Soup'.

Once upon a time a man was walking from one town to another. This was in the days before there were cars and buses. The roads were very bad and journeys took a very long time. The man walked many miles each day and he got very tired towards evening. Sometimes he stayed at *inns*—if he could find them; sometimes he slept in the open. It was an exhausting journey.

One evening the *traveller* arrived at a small village. It was a pretty little village but there was something about it which the traveller didn't know. The people in this village didn't like strangers. It wasn't a *friendly* village. The traveller suspected nothing. He looked round the village for an inn, but, of course, in a village like this he couldn't find such a thing. No one had an inn. No one wanted to look after strangers. The villagers looked at the traveller through their windows, but they didn't open their doors. They all drew their curtains and pretended they hadn't seen anyone. It was very late and it was getting quite dark. The traveller knew he couldn't walk to the next village, so he decided to ask one of the villagers to give him a bed and some food for the night. He was going to pay for both, of course. He knocked at one door and then at another, but no one opened. The villagers pretended they hadn't heard anything.

This is very strange, the traveller thought. Either all these houses are empty, or the people here just don't like strangers. I wonder what I can do to persuade them to open their doors. He banged on the doors and shouted, but no one paid any attention. The poor traveller got very tired indeed. Finally, he came to the last house in the village. It was a tiny place and it didn't look at all friendly. He knocked at the door, but no one answered. Then he shouted, "Please give me a bed for the night. I'm very tired. I'll pay you well."

An old woman lived in this house. She heard the words "I'll pay you well" and decided to open the door.

"You are very kind," the traveller said to the old woman when he had settled down. "I'm very hungry, have you got anything for me to eat?"

"No," the old woman said. "There's no food in this house. I've given you a bed for the night and that's enough. Now please don't bother me."

The traveller tried to persuade the old woman to give him some food, but she refused. In the end he said, "I'm going outside for a moment," and he went out of the door. He soon returned with a small stone. "I know you haven't any food in the house," he said, "and I know you can't give me anything to eat, but I'm really very hungry. Do you mind if I boil this stone in water to make some soup? I remember an old recipe for stone soup which my mother gave me." The old woman looked at the stone and she looked at the man. "Stone soup?" she laughed. "All right, you can make some over the fire."

The man put the stone in a pot which he filled with water and put it over the fire. Soon the water began to boil and he tasted it. "Mm," he said. "It's very nice. It just needs a little *flavouring*." He looked round the kitchen and saw some cabbage leaves. "Do you mind if I put these in the pot?" The woman didn't answer, so he put them in. Then he tasted the soup again. "Mm," he said. "Not bad, but it still needs some flavouring." He looked round the kitchen and found half a chicken. "Do you mind if I put this in?" the woman said nothing, so the man put it in. Then he tasted it again. "It's improving," he said, "but it still needs a bit more flavouring. He looked round the kitchen and found some onions and some potatoes which he put into the soup. Then he added some salt and pepper.

"It's almost ready," the man said. "Just a little more salt." Then he put some in a plate. "It's amazing what you can make just from a stone and some water. Would you like to try some?" he asked the woman.

The soup smelt delicious, so the woman wanted to try it.

"It's delicious, isn't it?" the man repeated.

And of course, she agreed!

Get Up and Shut the Door (Part 1)

This is an old story which was written as a *ballad* in England many hundreds of years ago. The story is in two parts. It's called 'Get Up and Shut the Door'.

There was once a farmer called Geoffrey who lived with his wife, Meg. They were quite a happy *couple*, but like most couples they quarrelled

137

occasionally. Sometimes their arguments lasted a very long time. You see, they were both *strong-willed* people. When they made up their minds to do something, they did it.

Geoffrey and Meg had a small piece of land. The land was owned by a rich lord. Remember, all this happened several hundred years ago and in those days, all the land was owned by rich lords and the people had to work on the land and had to give part of their *crop* to their masters. And that's how it was with Geoffrey. He grew crops on the land and he grew vegetables, too. He kept a few animals as well. Part of the crop had to be given to the owner of the land. Some bad farmers never had enough food for themselves. But Geoffrey was a good farmer. He gave part of his crop to his master and he never complained. He always had plenty of food for himself and his wife. His children had grown up and gone to live in another village, so life wasn't too difficult.

And, of course, Meg was a good housewife. She knew how to make a little go a long way. Her house was always tidy. The floors were washed regularly so they were always clean. The little furniture they had was regularly dusted. Everything was *spotless*. Meg was a good cook, too. Bread was baked on Fridays, but sometimes Meg made a few cakes which her husband liked very much.

Meg was neat and tidy. But although Geoffrey was a good farmer, he wasn't a very tidy person. He often came into the house with muddy shoes and this led to quarrels.

One day, Meg baked a lot of bread. While she was baking, she thought, I'll give Geoffrey a surprise. I'll bake him some cakes and tarts. You can imagine how the kitchen smelt at the end of the day. The bread had been baked and Meg was still busy. She was baking cakes and tarts. There was a delicious smell of fresh bread and cakes.

At about six o'clock Geoffrey came in from the fields. It had been a very bad day for him. The weather had been very bad indeed. It was wet and windy outside and Geoffrey was in a very bad temper. He pushed open the kitchen door and then shut it again. He came into the kitchen *roughly*. He didn't even say "Good evening" to Meg and he didn't even say "What a nice smell" or anything like that. But he did remember to take his muddy boots off.

"Good evening, my dear," Meg said. "I've been baking."

"Mm," Geoffrey said roughly, "I can see that." Geoffrey sat down at the kitchen table opposite his wife. Meg was sitting at the table, too. She was rolling out some *pastry*. "I've had a bad day," Geoffrey complained. "The weather has been awful. It's been raining and it's been windy." Just as he said that, the back door blew open.

"I'm sorry to hear that, my dear," Meg said. "It has been a bad day—I can see that. Look the wind has blown open the kitchen door. Get up and shut it please or the kitchen will get dirty."

"Get up and shut it yourself," Geoffrey said rudely.

"But my hands are covered with pastry. And, *anyway*, you didn't shut the door properly when you came in. That's why it was opened by the wind."

"Nonsense," Geoffrey shouted crossly. "I shut it properly. Of course I shut it properly. It's your kitchen so you can shut the door. Get up and shut it." He banged the table with his fist when he said this.

Now Meg got very angry. "Oh, it's my kitchen, is it?" she said. "I've been in here all day baking bread and cakes for your tea. I'm hot and tired. You come in, bad-tempered as usual. You don't even say 'Good evening' or anything. You don't even notice I've been baking. You push the kitchen door so that it doesn't shut and then it's blown open by the wind. Then you tell ME to shut it. ME! Shut it yourself!"

"I certainly will not," Geoffrey shouted.

"All right," Meg replied. "The first one to speak, must get up and shut the door. Do you agree?"

"That suits me fine," Geoffrey said. "It can stay open all night *for all I care!*"

Get Up and Shut the Door (Part 2)

Do you remember the first part of this story? Do you remember how Geoffrey and Meg quarrelled? They agreed that the first one to speak would have to get up and shut the door, didn't they?

Meg sat quietly at one end of the table. She didn't make any more cakes. Geoffrey sat quietly at the other end of the table. *Now and then*, he *rubbed* his beard crossly. He was very bad-tempered. The wind blew into the kitchen. It brought in leaves and dust. The kitchen became very cold. Soon it began to get quite dark outside, but Meg and Geoffrey sat opposite each other. Neither of them spoke.

Meanwhile, two tramps were walking along the road. They were both very hungry and they were looking for a house where they might get some food.

"Look at that house there," one of them said as they passed Geoffrey's house. "There's no light in the window, but perhaps we can get some food."

"We'd better knock at the door," the second tramp said.

The tramps went to the back door. It should have been shut, but, of course, it was wide open. "That's unusual," one of the tramps said. "The door's wide open. Anybody home?" he called.

But there was no answer.

"Let's go in then," the second tramp said.

It was quite dark in the kitchen, but the tramps soon saw Geoffrey and Meg in the darkness. The first tramp spoke to Meg. "Good evening, Mrs," he said. "We were passing and we thought we might get a little food. There's a lovely smell in this kitchen. You've been baking, I suppose. May we have one little cake each?"

Meg looked at the two tramps. They were very dirty and their clothes were torn. They were both very ugly. They looked very unpleasant indeed. But, of course, she didn't answer the tramp's question.

"She doesn't seem to mind if we have a few cakes," the second tramp said. "Look! There they are. Mm. They smell delicious. Here, have one."

The tramps had one each. "May we have another?" the first man asked.

"She doesn't seem to mind," the second man said. So they had another. And another. And another. And another after that, until they had eaten them all.

"I'm already feeling better," the first tramp said. "But it would be nice if we could have a bit of light. It's so dark in here. See if you can get the good lady to light this lamp for us."

The second tramp tried to get Meg to light the lamp in the kitchen, but she didn't move. So he turned to Geoffrey. "Would you light it for me please, sir?" he asked. But Geoffrey didn't move.

"You can't make them light it," the first tramp said. "You'd better light it yourself."

As soon as the lamp was lit the kitchen looked very bright. The first tramp held the lamp under Meg's nose, then he held it under Geoffrey's nose. "They look a funny couple, don't they?" he said. He gave Geoffrey a hard *pinch*. Geoffrey looked at the tramp angrily, but he didn't move.

"Well, he's not dead," the tramp said.

"Those cakes were good, but I'm still rather hungry," the second tramp said. "I'd rather eat meat. I always prefer meat to cakes. Let's look for some."

They looked round the kitchen and found some nice salt meat which Meg had been saving for the winter and they both sat down on the floor and ate it.

"The salt in that meat has made me thirsty. We'd better try and find something to drink."

"There's some milk in this cupboard," the second tramp said. "And there's some beer. Which would you rather have?"

"You have the milk, and I'll have the beer," the first tramp said.

"They are a funny couple," the second tramp said. "We've eaten their food and drunk their drink and they haven't said anything."

"We can make them say something," the first tramp said. "You cut off the old man's beard and I'll kiss his wife."

The second tramp took a knife and went towards Geoffrey, but Geoffrey didn't move. When he saw the first tramp walking towards Meg, he jumped up angrily. "Get out of my house, both of you!" he cried and he *seized* both tramps by their collars and threw them out of the house.

"And while you're up, dear," Meg said with a big smile on her face, "you can shut that door."

And that's just what Geoffrey did.

The Day Father was Arrested

This is a change from traditional stories. It's a story father likes telling. This is how he usually tells it:

I got home from work at about 5.30. It was rather cold, I remember, and I was wearing a hat and coat. As it was rather windy, I had turned up my collar so that you could hardly see my face. I went towards the front door, as usual. I put my hand in my pocket to get my key, but I couldn't find it. I searched everywhere for it and then remembered that I had left it on my desk in the office. It didn't really matter. I knew that Betty was at home and the children must have got back from school, so I knocked at the door. There was no answer so I knocked again. I continued knocking at the door for some time and I was getting annoyed. I hate waiting for a long time. Then I remembered something Betty had said that morning. At breakfast time, she had said to the children, "I want to go shopping this afternoon, children. Perhaps you'd like to come shopping with me when you get back home from school." And they had said "yes", of course. Shopping is fun for them, though I always find it an exhausting business.

Anyway, as I was saying, I realized that I was stuck. There was only one thing to do: I must get in through a window. I looked up and noticed that one of the upstairs windows was open. I was very lucky. I had thought I might have to break a window, but that wasn't necessary. So I went to the back of the house to get our ladder. It's a very tall ladder and it's pretty difficult carrying it, I can tell you. I nearly fell over once or twice and I said one or two bad things. But there was no one there to hear me swearing—or so I thought!

I put the ladder against the wall and began climbing towards the open window. I must have looked funny in my hat and my coat, climbing up a ladder. I was carrying my bag, too. I suppose it all looked very suspicious to anybody watching.

I was so pleased when I reached the window that I dived in head first. I shut the window behind me. I was in our bedroom, so I decided I would change my clothes and then go downstairs and watch the news on television.

Suddenly I heard a *siren* in the distance. There must have been an accident somewhere, I thought. I looked out of the window and saw a police car coming up the street, its blue light *flashing*. It must have been in our street, I thought. I wonder who it could be? I watched the police car coming up the street and then I saw it stop. It stopped right outside my house! That's funny, I thought, perhaps there's been a robbery, or something. I wonder who's in trouble. I saw two policemen get out and then I saw them coming towards my house. I wonder what they want, I thought, as I put on my old trousers.

Then I heard them knocking at my front door. I'd better answer it, I thought and I went downstairs. "Good evening," I said. "What can I do for you?"

The officers were very rude. "Are you the only person in this house?" one of them asked.

"Yes," I said.

"Then you'd better come with us. You used this ladder to get into the house, didn't you? You'd better come to the station with us— quietly."

"I'd rather stay here, if you don't mind," I said. "I can easily explain. You see my wife and my children have gone shopping and . . ."

One of the police officers interrupted me. "You can explain everything at the station," he repeated. "Now are you coming quietly or not?"

Of course, I was very annoyed and I showed it, so the officers took me by the arms—one on each side—and almost carried me to their car.

As I was being taken to the car, I happened to look up at the house next door and happened to see a figure standing beside the curtains and looking down at me. I looked at the ladder outside my house and *put two and two together*: I realized what had happened. Mrs Gasbag had seen everything and had called the police. She was minding her own business, as usual. I had a job explaining it all at the station! I've never forgotten my key since then, I can tell you!

King Alfred and the Cakes

Nobody knows if this story is true, but it is a story which the writers of history books enjoy telling. It is a well-known story about an English King called Alfred. Alfred was a very famous English King who was born in 849 and who died in 899. He is usually referred to as "Alfred the Great" because of all the wonderful things he did while he was King. He started many schools and *monasteries*; he encouraged teachers to come to England; he had many *Latin* books *translated* into English (or Anglo-Saxon as it then was); he had many ships built and he *created* quite a large army. Although Alfred did all these important things, he was a very simple man and his people loved him. This story about the cakes shows us how simple he was.

While Alfred was King, the *Danes* kept coming across the sea in boats. They burnt villages and fought against the local people. England was *at war* all the time and King Alfred was in charge of the army. After one big *battle* King Alfred suddenly found himself alone. Many of his men had been killed and he had to find the rest of his army. He started walking through the woods and across fields and after walking for many hours, he felt extremely tired. Suddenly he saw a small farmhouse and he went towards it.

He knocked at the door and waited. At last a woman opened the door and asked the King what he wanted. She didn't know he was the King, of course. She looked at him suspiciously. His clothes were torn and dirty and his face and hands were dirty, too.

"Excuse me troubling you, madam," the King

said, "but I'm very tired and hungry. May I come in and rest please? Perhaps I could also have something to eat."

The woman continued to look at the King suspiciously. Somehow, he didn't look like a *beggar*. "All right," she said at last. "You can come in and sit by the fire. You can have something to eat, too. But you'll have to pay for it."

"I'm sorry," the King said. "I'm not carrying any money at present, but I can arrange to have some money sent to you . . ."

The woman interrupted him. "It's all right," she said. "You can pay for your food by working for it. I'm just making some cakes at the moment, so while sitting by the fire you can look after the cakes and take them off the fire when they're ready."

Entering the house, the King went into the kitchen and sat by the nice warm fire. The good woman brought him some food which he ate hungrily. After eating the food he began watching the cakes which were on a metal tray over the fire. He watched the cakes and kept looking into the fire and he got very sleepy. He couldn't help falling asleep—it just happened.

Well, you can imagine what happened to the cakes. There was a smell of burning and the woman rushed into the kitchen and *roughly* woke up the King. She was very angry with him. "I allowed you to sit by my warm fire. I gave you food to eat and all I asked you to do was to look after my cakes. It was such an easy job, even a child could have done it. And look what you've done! You fell asleep and all my cakes are burnt. They're just not fit to eat now. I shall have to throw them away."

"I'm very sorry," the King said. "Truly, I am. I was looking . . ."

Just then there was a loud knock at the door. The woman opened it and some *soldiers* spoke to her. "We're looking for the King," they said. "We know he came this way. Is he here please?"

Just then they saw the King. "Oh, Your Majesty," they said, "we have come to lead you back to your men."

"The King!" the woman cried. She fell on her knees. "Oh, Your Majesty, please *forgive* me for being so hard and unkind! How could I know? Oh please forgive me."

"You were not unkind," the King said. "You gave me food and let me rest. I must apologize to you for being so careless. Thank you for letting me come into your house, and I am sorry for burning your lovely cakes."

And then he left the house and went back to his army to continue fighting against the Danes.

Mother Passes Her Driving Test

Mother has been learning to drive for some time now. But father is not a very good teacher. He always complains about mother's driving. He's impatient and sometimes he shouts. He's afraid mother might crash—that's the real trouble.

Mother was very nervous last week because she was going to take her driving test. "I'd better give you one or two lessons before the test," father said. "I think you still need some more practice."

"You only make me nervous, Jim," mother said. "I'm getting better at driving . . ."

"But you still make mistakes," father interrupted.

"And so do you!" mother said.

Father *blushed*. He knew that mother was right. Only the other day he had nearly turned into a one-way street. It was mother who prevented him from turning: she noticed it before he did.

They argued for a bit, but mother knew she needed some more practice so she went driving with father. "I'll keep my eyes shut," father said.

"Don't do that, Jim," mother answered. "What's the use of coming with me if you keep your eyes shut?"

"I was only joking," father said. "I'd be frightened of keeping my eyes shut. I want to see where you're going."

Mother got behind the *driving-wheel* and father sat beside her. "I'm looking forward to driving this afternoon," she said as she started the engine. The car jumped.

"It's still *in gear!*" father cried. "The first thing you do is to check if it's in gear. You do that before starting the engine. You should know that by now."

"Well who left it in gear, I'd like to know!" mother answered.

"I did," father said.

"Well you shouldn't've."

"There's no law against parking a car in gear," father said.

"If you're going to argue, I'm not going to drive at all," mother replied.

"Well start driving, then," father said, "so we can stop arguing."

Mother started the car *smoothly* and she *changed gears* without having any trouble at all. She drove the car very well indeed—even father had to admit that mother had driven very well. "You've done very well," he said.

"Of course I have," mother said. "Women are better drivers than men. They aren't so impatient. They don't get so cross. They don't swear at the other drivers on the road. They are responsible people. They have young children to look after."

While saying all these things, mother was driving the car into the garage and she nearly hit the wall.

"Look out!" father shouted. "Responsible

people! You ought to look where you're going."

"I was looking where I was going, but you make me cross."

"I only congratulated you on driving so well," father said.

"I don't mean you. I mean men. They're always criticizing women drivers, but they often drive badly themselves."

"Now let's not start arguing again," father said.

The next day mother took her test. She was dreadfully nervous, but she passed. She was very pleased when she came home that evening. The whole family congratulated her on passing. Mother was so pleased she insisted on taking them all out for a meal to celebrate.

"I'm glad you succeeded in passing, Betty," father said. "I'm glad because I won't have to teach you any more. I hate teaching."

"And I'm glad you won't have to teach me any more," mother said.

"And we're glad, too," Sue said, "because we won't have to listen to any more arguments."

"Arguments?" father asked.

"What arguments?" mother asked.

"Arguments," Sue repeated.

"We never argue," father said, "at least only sometimes." And he gave mother a kiss.

"Only sometimes," Sue said. And she gave mother a kiss, too. "Congratulations on passing, mum," she said. "You're the best driver in the world."